PLAYING BLACKJACK

with

GOD

A PSYCHIC MEDIUM AND A LIFE COACH TEAM UP TO ASK GOD THE TRUTH OF THIS LIFE, AND GET SURPRISING ANSWERS

Laurie Gregg *and* Kellie deRuyter

Published by Divine Being Communications
769 Broadway, Suite 1168
New York, NY 10003

For permission requests, please email:

inquiries@playingblackjackwithgod.com

Printed in the USA
ISBN 978-1-7375315-0-0 eBook
ISBN 978-1-7375315-1-7 Paperback

SOURCE MATERIAL

All meaningful conversations between the authors and Divine Source/God in this book were extracted from verbatim transcriptions of recordings. In those recordings, Laurie relayed precisely what she heard, word-for-word. Everything meaningful the authors said about themselves and their own lives was their true perspective.

The non essential wording in those conversations has been "cleaned up" a bit for ease in reading, however, in no way was the important wording, meaning, message, or context of any communication from Divine Source/God changed.

For entertainment purposes, the lighthearted storyline that supports the meaningful conversations is pure fiction interwoven with a few actual events and real people. In both the real conversations and the fictional storyline, some identifying names and non-essential details have been changed to protect the privacy of individuals.

This book is dedicated to our sons, for all the love, laughter, and joy they've brought into our lives

CONTENTS

ACKNOWLEDGEMENTS

The process of writing this book was many times more complicated than that of an ordinary book, and spanned many years. We would like to thank our sons and significant others for their unending patience and understanding during those years. You guys all rock!

We'd like to thank the editors who so generously donated their time, because they believed in us: My mother Barbara deRuyter, and our friend, Liz Fisch.

Special thanks go to Laurie Lawson from the bottom of our hearts. Her reviews are always very candid and she was the first to read and review our book. Her enthusiasm, delight, and support brought tears to our eyes and helped us realize how many people's lives we could truly change.

We'd also like to express our gratitude and thanks to Starr Fuentes for all of her psychic advice regarding moving the book forward.

"What's happening . . . what the hell is happening?"

"Oh my God, another plane just hit the second tower!"

Laurie's husband Keith, a New York fireman, was right in the middle of one of the most tragic disasters in history. Laurie supplied him with vital information on the events transpiring via cell phone, all the while praying that her husband would come home alive to her and their 6-month-old son.

He did not come home for days, but he did come home. Many of his buddies and co-workers did not. Wretched and with a sore heart, he called upon his friends who had lost their lives that terrible day to come in and speak to him through Laurie, his wife. Laurie had the ability to hear spirit clearly, after attending four years of intense psychic training to hone that natural ability.

"You know I always wanted to be a show-off, and look, Rudy Giuliani is coming to my funeral," joked one.

"The sky is falling, the sky is falling," mocked another,

also joking, who was in the lobby of World Trade Center One when it came down. He claimed to have felt nothing.

He didn't even realize he was dying at the time; it only dawned on him later.

One fireman was very confused, stuck without realizing he was dead. Keith tried to explain: "You know you remember going into the trade center. It was terrorists that hit, the two towers crumbled down, and you were inside. You died. You're actually dead at the moment."

"No way," his friend said, who thought Keith was playing a joke on him.

"How do you feel right now?" Keith asked.

"Like I drank too many beers."

"If you look around, you'll see a light way in the distance. You can go to that light . . . and know that you're a great hero now."

Each one had a story. Each one was concerned about grieving loved ones left behind. Each one found closure before they moved on, thanks to Laurie's amazing ability to hear what they had to say.

My name is Kellie deRuyter, and I've been friends with Laurie Gregg for almost two decades now. Laurie has been a professional psychic for over 20 years, using her talent to help clients converse with their spirit guides, angels, and other high-level beings. She hears spirits, *all* spirits, no matter what level or plane of existence they are on, word-for-word—as though she were having a conversation on the phone. This book is the story of how we discovered she could even hear and speak to God/Source/Spirit, or however you choose to name and acknowledge Universal Intelligence. It's also full of never-before-heard information from that source on how the game of life *actually* works, which we believe will help you—the reader—feel more hopeful, less fearful, and even have more fun in life!

This is the story of how we had to come to terms with the fact that God/Source/Spirit was a real, individual intelligence—and I'll even dare to say an intelligence with a personality—who could converse with us, through Laurie, as well as be all that IS. Most importantly, this book contains, word for word, what that individual intelligence wants the world to know here and now, during one of the most important times in history.

When I first met Laurie, in addition to working with a select clientele, she was working as a psychic consultant for a government allied with the US, helping prevent war and terrorism. Through her work, more than one significant threat to the US and Europe was found and neutralized. For example, a terrorist attempting to plant a bomb in a midtown Manhattan subway was apprehended as a direct result of the information she provided.

Of course, I didn't know any of that until we became friends, but I was already so impressed with her ability it didn't surprise me in the least. After getting chills and goosebumps upon seeing her picture in a magazine I picked up while waiting at the chiropractor's, I felt compelled to contact her for a reading. How the angels made sure we became friends is a story for another day. The best story, the one that will help bring you peace in these uncertain times, is the one where we talk to God: right here in this book.

Although every verbal interaction with God really happened and we personally believe we were speaking directly with Source, Laurie and I recommend you consider the information provided on its own merits. It's meant to help you live a happier, more fulfilled life. However, even if God said it, he'd be the first to say if it doesn't work for you, let it go. So, ask yourself: Does it make sense to you? Does it resonate with you? Does it work for you? Does it help you reduce fear and anxiety, have more fun, and live a happier life? If it does, great! If it doesn't, that's okay too. Just metaphorically toss anything that doesn't contribute to your happiness and well-being.

You may also wonder, why did he choose us? According to him, it's because we're ordinary. We're just like everyone else. He didn't want to speak directly to kings, queens, presidents, spiritual leaders, personal growth gurus, or to any prominent person for something like this, because the "regular person" can't relate to those people. The two of us have had our share of hard knocks in life, and we haven't always been the most enlightened about them either. That's exactly what he wanted.

In fact, when Laurie first began hearing God, she was very angry with him, and continued to be angry for a while. I wasn't too thrilled with my life either, or the direction the world was headed. We both demanded answers, and we weren't concerned about being nice or politically correct. The gloves were off. That was just fine with him. Many people feel the way we did. He wanted to speak directly to those people, through Laurie. So if you are unhappy with your life, or disappointed in how the world is today, in this book we ask God himself the hard-hitting questions that you would if you had the chance. You'll finally get the *real* answers you've been waiting for.

Many people view life as a struggle. They are continually looking for the right partner, the right job, better health, more money; the list goes on and on. But they never seem to quite get to that place of peace and happiness they so strongly desire.

This book is meant to give you the opportunity to look at your life in a completely different way. To see the obstacles, challenges, and everyday events in the same way that God, or that your soul, sees them. When you see them in this dramatically different way, you'll be able to change them much more easily. And, if they don't change, this book contains the secret on how to be happy anyway. It's a win-win! You've gotta love that.

The information here is detailed, explicit, clear, and life changing. We hope that sharing it with you at this point in time will allow you to lead a happier and more fulfilling life.

PART I
THE GAME

CHAPTER 1

Early in the morning on August 29, 2005, Hurricane Katrina struck the Gulf Coast of the United States. When the storm made landfall, it had a Category 3 rating on the Saffir-Simpson Hurricane Scale—it brought sustained winds of 100-140 miles per hour—and stretched some 400 miles across. The storm itself did a great deal of damage, but its aftermath was catastrophic. Levee breaches led to massive flooding, and many people charged that the federal government was slow to meet the needs of the people affected by the storm. Hundreds of thousands of people in Louisiana, Mississippi and Alabama were displaced from their homes, and experts estimate that Katrina caused more than $100 billion in damage. More than 1,800 people died in the hurricane and its aftermath.

—A&E TELEVISION NETWORK

September 2005
New York City, New York

The kitchen table in the modest Manhattan apartment was really more of an end table with delusions of grandeur. Kellie lived in California, so when she visited her friend Laurie in New York City, she was astonished at the small size of the kitchen. Even though the size was typical for a Manhattan apartment, it amused her that the only place for the tiny wooden table was the entry hall.

The bright yellow and white kitchen was about the size of her twins' old plastic playhouse in the yard back home in Santa Cruz, Kellie thought as she slid into the chair with her plate of sizzling bacon and eggs. She could hear the muffled sound of traffic coming from the busy Manhattan street outside the apartment, punctuated by the occasional sound of a horn.

Laurie, who rented the apartment, was taking an unexpected call in the bedroom with the door closed. Although Kellie couldn't make out her words, she became alarmed at the tone of her friend's voice. Leaving her food untouched, Kellie frowned, concerned.

Suddenly the door opened and Laurie walked out into the living room, throwing the headset and phone down onto the overstuffed green couch and heading toward the kitchen. A mixture of conflicting emotions played across her face: confusion, anxiety, excitement, anticipation, and worry.

Kellie waited. It didn't take long. "I feel like my head's about to explode," Laurie exclaimed. "I can't believe what just happened!"

"What?" Kellie said, on cue.

"That was a representative of the US government. She

wants me to come work for them and do what I did three years ago, predicting terrorist attacks." She stopped in front of Kellie. "I'm so conflicted! I want so badly to do it, to help. And it's kind of exciting. My heart is beating double-time, and it's saying, 'yes, yes, yes!' but my brain is saying, 'no, no, no, you're crazy! You got out of that line of work because you had a child, remember? It's too dangerous.'"

She sighed and put her hands over her face. In a muffled voice, she said, "Of all days, I did not need this today. I'm already so upset about the hurricane and my family's home in Louisiana being flooded." She put her hands back down at her sides, took a deep breath and said, "I told her I'd get back to her next week. I just can't even think about that right now. I can only deal with one emotional upheaval at a time, and this week, it's my family and the hurricane."

"What can I do to help?" Kellie asked.

Laurie looked at her gratefully. "Just being here is enough. Thank you."

Laurie turned and walked into the kitchen, scooped some bacon and eggs onto a plate, and came back to the table. She sat down and picked up her fork, silently eating her breakfast. Kellie sat back and studied her friend's delicate features for a moment. "How *is* your family?" she asked finally, leaning forward again and picking up a piece of bacon. "I know you spoke to your mom earlier this morning." Kellie was well aware that Laurie's family in Louisiana had been missing for several days. In fact, Laurie had only just learned they were all safe the day before.

Laurie tucked a stray auburn curl behind her ear as she picked up her fork.

As she considered Kellie's question, she shrugged, then said with a touch of bitterness, "How is my family? About as well as you might expect when your home is under ten feet of water, you can't find your cherished pets, and you're not able to get anything to eat unless it comes in a can. My mom is worried sick about her cats, and she says she's had enough beans and Dinty Moore stew to last her a lifetime."

Kellie's voice softened in sympathy. "I'm so sorry."

Dark brown eyes flashing with anger, Laurie replied, "It's not your fault. You didn't personally send the hurricane to Louisiana to demolish my family home." She stabbed viciously at the eggs cooling on her plate, the fork clinking loudly as she scooped up a bite. She paused, eggs suspended in mid-air, and frowned. "I just wish I knew why these horrible things happen to innocent people who are simply minding their own business, trying to live a good life."

Kellie nodded in silent agreement, shifting her gaze to the window behind the table and looking pensively out at the dark gray September sky. It looked as though a storm was brewing. The hallway light was off. She looked down at her hands, noticing that her fair skin seemed darker in the cold light.

She sighed, absently running her fingers through her shoulder-length blonde hair.

Kellie's thoughts then drifted to Laurie's comment about bad things happening to innocent people. She thought of all the times she had tried to take a step forward toward building a career, or heck, even just a life, only to be stopped or delayed by the mysterious illness that had afflicted her and zapped her energy since she was seventeen years old. It had been so much harder for her to do what everyone else simply took for granted. It seemed a miracle she had even graduated from college, much less earned her personal coach certification and credentials. And starting a family? Definitely a miracle. She smiled at the thought of her eleven-year-old twin boys, and continued eating her breakfast.

After a silence broken only by the soft clinking of silverware, Laurie abruptly set a forkful of eggs back down on her plate, picking up the conversation again. "I'm not just talking about my family and the hurricane, either. I'm talking about my clients, who call with some of the most heart-wrenching stories. I want to help so much, but being a psychic doesn't mean I can fix everything." Her eyes clouded with sadness as she fixed her gaze on her plate.

Hearing the pain in her voice, Kellie sat back in the chair, looking solemnly at her friend. "I know," she said. "Aside from my frustration at my own challenges, I hear the same kinds of stories from the clients I coach. I can't fix everything either." She paused, reaching for her coffee and taking a slow sip. After a moment, she set the mug down with a decisive thump. "Well, you *are* the best darn psychic channel in town. You could channel the angels and we could ask *them* why horrible things happen to innocent people. It couldn't hurt, and we might hear something that makes us feel better."

Laurie sighed. "Maybe you're right." Taking another bite of her breakfast, she made a face at the cooling eggs. Then, suddenly making up her mind, she dropped her fork and pushed her plate away. "Let's do it. I don't feel much like eating anyway."

Startled, Kellie said, "All right, I'm game."

<h1 style="text-align:center">CHAPTER 2</h1>

New York City, New York

Laurie sat up straight. "Who should we call in? Archangel Metatron?"

Ramping up into high gear and abandoning manners, Kellie began eating quickly and said around a mouthful of bacon, "He *is* the angel who seems to know a little bit about everything. He's also always been there whenever we've needed anything."

"Okay, Metatron it is." Laurie pushed her chair back and got up from the table. Heading into the living room, she walked around the maple coffee table and plopped down on the couch.

Kellie watched as a momentary glimpse of pain crossed Laurie's face as her eyes settled on eleven-year-old Ben's unfinished model train set. He was with his dad for a few days and clearly she missed him terribly. She always scheduled as many work calls as she could while he was gone so she could spend more time with him when he was with her.

Laurie gave her head a shake to clear her thoughts. "Here goes." She closed her eyes, sank back into the couch, took a deep breath, and exhaled with a loud sigh.

Her chest rose and fell with soft whooshes as she took a few more slow, deep breaths. In that wonderfully soothing and melodic voice that Kellie loved, she began, "I'm bringing in white light laced with silver and gold, wrapping it all around me head to toe, all around you, all around my son Ben and all around your sons Aron and Kyle. I'm sure my home could use some light too, so I am sending it to each room and every corner."

She paused, and Kellie knew she was being thorough, completely surrounding everything with the protective light. Laurie was a stickler about that. Unlike some other psychics, she did not care for 'uninvited spirit guests,' so she always created a safe space with clear boundaries.

"Kellie's angel guides, my angel guides, come in and give me a signal to let me know you're here, please." After another pause, she said "They popped in and lightly tapped my head, so it feels a bit like it's a piece of popcorn in a popper. Guides, I'd like you to anchor us please, while we do this. Archangel Metatron, please come in and give me a signal." Then after a moment, she said, "He's here. I feel his presence like soft feathers lightly brushing my shoulders."

Kellie felt the same thrill she always felt, knowing she was in the presence of a very wise being. Swallowing her last bite, she stood up and grabbed Laurie's plate along with hers and dashed into the kitchen, unceremoniously dumping plates and eating utensils into the sink. The faucet made a rumbling sound as she turned it on, spraying water all over the dishes. She waited a moment, then turned it off, leaving them to soak. She raced to pull out her chair and move it into the living room, opposite Laurie, on the other side of the coffee table. She ran back and grabbed her coffee. In her usual mode of playful amusement, she set it down on the coffee table, plopped down in the chair and sat up with exaggerated attentiveness, holding perfectly still, hands folded in front of her, eyes fixed on Laurie. No matter how often she experienced it, hearing Laurie relay what the angels were saying *never* got boring.

Laurie cracked one eye open as if to say, 'Really?' She closed it again and began, "Metatron, we'd like to know why so many terrible things are always happening in the world, things that are devastating to people who don't seem to have done anything to deserve it. It just doesn't seem fair." She cocked her head, listening, then repeated out loud, "He says, 'That's a better question for God to answer. Why don't you ask him?'" Her eyes sprang open and she stared at Kellie, who stared back in astonishment.

After a stunned silence, Kellie said, "What?" She tried to wrap her brain around the question. "You don't mean the way we talk to you and the other angels of course, with him talking back to us. You mean in prayer, or something like that. Or by meditating and tapping into the source within us, which is what God really is, right? He's not actually an individual being, like you are."

Laurie closed her eyes again, then relayed Metatron's answer: "He's saying, 'He is the source within, it's true. But what makes you think he doesn't manifest as a single consciousness as well?'"

Laurie's eyes popped open again, with angry glints in them this time. "Oh, come on Metatron," she spit out, "If there really were a God who was a single individual, why would he let so many people suffer so much, all over the world, all the time? If there really were a being so almighty and all-powerful, where the hell is he when people need him?"

Kellie opened her mouth to speak, but when she saw that the angry glints in Laurie's eyes had turned to flames, she clamped it shut again. At this point, discretion was probably the wisest choice.

Laurie was clearly working herself up into a rant. Jumping up, she stormed around the table and across the room. "Let's say he does exist as an individual consciousness—which I doubt, by the way." She did an about face toward Kellie and held her index finger up in the air pointedly. "Does he really answer anyone's prayers, or is it just some big cosmic joke 'up there' that we people on earth *think* he helps us? Are all the angels hanging out on cloud nine chuckling about how deluded we are as they kick back and listen to the nightly harp recital?"

She walked back and grabbed the morning's freshly inked newspaper off the coffee table, the September first date displayed above the latest hurricane headline. She folded it in half and shook it at Kellie. "There's way more bad news than good. Just read the paper." She slammed the newspaper back down on the coffee table with a loud *thwack*. "I'll bet a lot of people who say they believe in God secretly wonder if there really is one, especially if something really bad has happened to them. For instance, what about a mother who has lost a child, even after praying a whole lot to God to save that child? I would think she'd be angry and wonder about God's existence, even if she didn't say anything out loud."

Kellie shrugged helplessly. She picked up her coffee, took a sip, and winced. "I hate cold coffee." She got up and went into the kitchen to microwave it. "You're so angry I don't think you'd talk to God," she said drily from the kitchen. "I think you'd just yell at him." She took several steps back to the doorway of the kitchen and leaned casually against the doorjamb, arms crossed, amusement evident in her dark blue eyes. She watched Laurie as she waited for the coffee to heat.

Laurie glared at her friend. "And so what if I did? He deserves it. He's certainly not doing a very good job of helping us, if you ask me."

She closed her eyes for a moment, then relayed Metatron's words: "He's saying, 'You're right. There are a lot of people who question if there is a God, because so many things happen that they believe are awful. That's why I think you should talk to him. Ask him why he allows people to suffer. Get the straight scoop, so to speak.'"

Kellie's gaze turned incredulous. In the silence that followed, the microwave bell dinged. After a moment, she turned around, walked back into the kitchen and removed the coffee from the microwave. She shook her head. "I can't believe I'm hearing this. I can't believe we can just talk to God, the same way we talk to other spirits or angels."

Laurie said to Metatron, "So, you're suggesting that the same way I say 'Hey, Metatron, come on in,' or 'Hey, whichever angel or guide I want to speak to, come on in,' I can just say, 'Yo, God, come on in and talk to us?'"

"That's exactly what I'm suggesting," he said. "In fact, I have a message for you, directly from God himself. Interested?"

Laurie froze, her eyes flying open again. It was the proverbial "deer in the headlights" look.

Standing in the doorway again, Kellie couldn't help bursting into laughter.

Coffee sloshed over the side of the cup, burning her hand. "Ouch!" she exclaimed. Switching the cup to her other hand, she wiped the wet hand on her jeans, still amused. "Do I detect a bit of trepidation?"

"Oh no," Laurie said sarcastically. "Calling in and speaking to *God*? To the being who's supposed to have created the whole *world* and everyone in it? Source *itself*? Why would I be nervous about that?"

"Hmm, I see your point. I'm a little nervous myself. Still," she held the coffee cup high in the air, saluting Laurie with one eyebrow cocked in sardonic amusement. "The gauntlet has been thrown down. How can we not?"

Laurie gulped. Then, her voice laced with misgiving, she said, "Okay Metatron, let's hear it."

CHAPTER 3

New York City, New York

"He says if you meet him tonight at nine o'clock on Bourbon Street in the French Quarter in New Orleans, he'll answer your questions there."

Surprise replaced the amusement on Kellie's face. She stood up straight.

"Wait. Laurie only hears the spirits and angels. You mean we'll get to see him as well?"

"This is a special circumstance, so yes, he's going to meet you in person, and you'll get to speak with him directly, both of you," Metatron said.

Laurie put her hands on her hips and responded to him, saying, "Well, special circumstance or not, we can't just hop on a plane and fly to New Orleans. It's an underwater wreck right now after the hurricane, and besides, plane tickets cost money."

"And just what would we say at the airport gate?" Kellie asked, lifting her eyebrow again. Then she batted her lashes. "'Oh, excuse us,'" she said in a sugary sweet voice, widening her eyes to look innocent. "God told us to meet him on Bourbon Street because he's going to answer our questions in person, so you need to let us into the city?"

Laurie rolled her eyes. "They'd let us in, all right. They'd let us directly in to the nearest psychiatric facility."

"Well, this is God we're talking about," Metatron continued. "He's offering the express route. He'll get you past all those minor difficulties. Just make sure you're here in this room tonight before 9, and then ask him to come in, just as you would any of the rest of us. He'll take it from there."

Laurie frowned. "How will I know if it's really God?"

Sounding amused, he said, "Who else would have the nerve to pretend to be God?

No one, trust me. But when you two get to New Orleans, look into his eyes," he suggested to her. "You'll know. In the meantime, I know you both have work calls scheduled today. Kellie, get your coaching calls done, and Laurie, do your psychic calls. Then you'll be ready to meet God tonight."

"How many coaching calls do you have today, Kellie?" Laurie asked.

"Five. How many psychic calls do you have?"

"Four, but two of them are going to be long. How 'bout if I go into my bedroom and do mine in there, and you do yours out here in the living room on your cell phone?"

"Sounds perfect, although I'm glad I'm good at focusing, or I'd never be able to do them, thinking about tonight!"

"I know. I'm glad I only have to repeat what the angels say, or I'd never be able to concentrate either! Thanks Metatron."

"You're very welcome. Now get ready for your calls, you two."

It was dark outside, and the two women were excited, but nervous. Too nervous to be hungry, they had skipped dinner. They were waiting in the living room for nine o'clock when it would finally be time to call in God. They still had no idea how they were getting to New Orleans, but figured they would find out soon enough. Laurie's stereo was on low, playing the latest soft rock hits.

"How did your calls go today?" Laurie sat on the floor by the partially constructed train set, combing through the loose pile of track, looking for just the right piece.

"Pretty well." Kellie was laying down on the couch, hands behind her head, propped up on one of the throw pillows. She turned her head toward Laurie. "I have an executive client who took a new job and found herself in the middle of an 'old boys club' situation. All the other execs are men and they treat her horribly. Needless to say, she's *not* 'in the club.'"

Laurie spotted the piece of track she wanted and reached over to pick it up. "Really? Wow, that's surprising. We are in the 21st century, after all."

Kellie rolled onto her side, grabbed the pillow and punched it a couple of times to fluff it up, then tucked it under her head again. "I know. But this is a manufacturing industry that is still male-dominated, and she just happens to be an expert in the field so she's the only woman. At any rate, they are so mean to her she told me she cries every day in the car on her way to work."

Laurie looked up at her, balancing the piece of track on her right palm. "That's awful, poor thing. So what happened when you coached her?"

"Oh, I lit a fire under her. Reminded her how awesome she was, how lucky they were to have her, and got her back in touch with what a kick-ass executive she was.

I inspired her to stand up for herself. Then I role-played with her, so she could find the perfect words and practice setting clear boundaries with them so they would back off."

"Sounds like you really helped her."

"Well, she got on the call feeling miserable and left it feeling fabulous. So now we'll see if she can hang onto that and give those chauvinists a run for their money. I think she will."

Laurie snapped the piece of track into place with an audible 'click'. "I bet she will, too. With you in her corner, how can she not?"

Kellie smiled. "Thanks. How about you? How did your calls go today?"

Laurie turned back to face her and crossed her legs on the floor, Indian style. She twisted her fingers together nervously. "I had one that was pretty intense. It was a woman who's done in vitro fertilization a few times and failed to get pregnant, and she's out of money. She has one egg left, one last chance, and if it doesn't work, she's done." She took a deep breath and let it out. "No kids."

"Wow. My heart goes out to her," Kellie said with feeling. "I've been there, and it *is* intense. There's so much riding on it. I'm so lucky it worked for me."

Laurie looked even more worried. "I know. You *were* lucky, and I *really* want this for her. But listen to this: The doctor had her scheduled to do it two days from now, and the angels said to cancel it, that it wouldn't work because she was too stressed out. They told her to wait a month to do it, and then it would be successful."

Kellie sat up on the couch and put her feet on the ground. "Oh my god! What did she say?"

"She was worried about going against the doctor, and of course I was nervous too, but I told her: 'The angels are right 95 percent of the time. I would absolutely go with what they say.' So she did. She said she was going to cancel the appointment and reschedule it for a month from now."

"Well, I've got my fingers crossed for her," Kellie said earnestly, holding up both hands with fingers crossed.

"Me, too!" Laurie said just as earnestly, holding both her hands up with fingers crossed as well.

They held their hands up together like that for a few more moments, then dropped them back into their laps. Laurie glanced at her watch. "Oh wow, it's almost nine o'clock!" She jumped up. Kellie stood up as well, and they faced each other nervously in the middle of the living room.

"What do I say to call him in? 'Yo God?' I feel silly just asking God to come in," Laurie said.

"Try it and see what happens," Kellie said encouragingly. "You've already brought in the light and done the prep to bring in the angels today on your calls. Just do what you always do, ask for a signal."

Laurie looked as though she was about to base jump off a cliff and wasn't at all certain the parachute was going to open. She drew in a couple of extra-deep breaths, blowing them out with loud exhales. She squared her shoulders in preparation. Finally, she said, "Yo God, will you please come in and give me a signal?"

CHAPTER 4

New York City, New York

The clock on the wall chimed once to announce it was on the hour. Kellie glanced at the hands and saw it was nine o'clock. Then, something caught her eye across the room and she sucked in her breath sharply. The startled sound caused Laurie to turn around to see what she was looking at. A moment before, the brown door separating the living room and the master bedroom had been clearly visible and slightly ajar. Now, a large, shining white door with a bright silver doorknob stood in the doorway instead, firmly closed. A beautiful, soft humming sound filled the room. Excited, Kellie said, "Okay, now that's what I call a signal!"

Laurie's mouth opened in astonishment, but no words came out. She just sat there staring.

Kellie jumped up and raced over to the door, then stopped, studying the new doorway. She reached out and touched it with her fingertips. Quick as lightning, a pleasant tingling sensation ran through her fingers, streaming up her arms and circling throughout her body. She jumped back. "Wow." She hugged herself, feeling the sensations ebb. "Well, it's solid."

Laurie blinked and pulled herself together. "Try opening it."

Kellie backed away from the door and swept her hand in a gesture that invited Laurie to be her guest. "You first."

"Fine. I'll go first. We'll probably just see the bedroom on the other side anyway."

♦ ♦ ♦ ♦

He knew the two women wanted answers. He also knew that many others on earth wanted those answers as well, so he had decided to give them what they wanted.

He contemplated the dark and deserted street. The endless stretch of filthy water enveloped the main thoroughfare and cross streets as far as the eye could see. Moonlight from the nearly full moon reflected off the greasy surface of the water, highlighting colored bits of garbage floating gently in the still night. The rancid odor of oil and garbage wafted through the humid air, without even the hint of a breeze to relieve the smell.

Trucks were strewn about with no regard for curbs or other such niceties: trucks with suction pumps, black garbage removal trucks, white power restoration trucks and a variety of pickup trucks in various colors. The deserted shopfronts cast long shadows in the moonlight, and a bar sign hung upside down at an angle, dangling forlornly by one chain. A café stood on the corner, door slightly ajar.

The water rose high enough to almost cover the wheels of the beat-up old pickup truck with peeling blue paint. He sat on the tailgate, swinging his legs in the water, waiting. The quiet splashing of his rubber boots was the only sound that broke the silence.

He'd wanted to appear as down-to-earth as possible, so he'd chosen to wear tattered blue jeans and a faded black and red checkered flannel shirt. The sleeves were rolled up to his elbows. He figured he looked a vital, healthy, 75-ish, give or take a few years. His face and arms were tanned. His medium-short salt-and-pepper hair was fashionably spiky on top. He'd chosen facial features which were pleasant but unremarkable. He had assumed a wise and benevolent expression. It was exactly the look he'd been aiming for.

There was nothing he could do about his eyes, however, and that was fine with him. He knew they were arresting. They were a deep brown and were so full of love, life, and compassion, it left no doubt at all as to who looked out from behind them. He was well aware that once people looked into his eyes, it was hard for them to look away and it became difficult for them to remember what they had just been thinking. It was usually much easier for them to simply lose themselves in the intensity of his regard.

It was time. He raised his hand slightly, and a glowing white doorway appeared, rising from the water in the street about ten feet away. It hummed softly.

He watched as the two women emerged from the doorway, holding their gaze once they caught sight of him and noting their expressions of disgust as they waded toward him through the oily mess. The door and the lovely hum vanished, leaving only the sound of their shoes splashing as they approached. They stopped in front of him, standing there awkwardly for a few seconds.

"How do we know you're really God?" Laurie said finally, an odd mixture of haughtiness and uncertainty in her voice.

"*Well, you did ask me to come.*"

"Yes, but how do we know it's really you, and not someone—or something— pretending to be you instead?"

"*Look into my eyes,*" he said.

So they did. Eventually, Laurie nodded. She and Kellie exchanged a wordless glance, in silent agreement. Both of them just intuitively recognized God/Source. Then Laurie's haughtiness disappeared and uncertainty took over. "Why are we here? This is a strange place to meet you."

"*I thought it was fitting. After all, you're unhappy with the fact that I've allowed all of this to happen.*" With one long sweep of his hand, he encompassed the shadows of the empty shops, storefronts and bars. Then he jumped down into the water with a decisive splash.

Pointing at the café on the corner, he said, "*Why don't we go in there and have a seat?*"

"Fine," Laurie said, the haughtiness back. "You're the boss."

He raised an eyebrow at her but said nothing. He simply led the way through the water to the corner, up the steps and into the café.

As the odd party trudged single file through the door, the dim moonlight filtering through the windows allowed Kellie to see that the café had been looted. It was a small hole-in-the-wall dive, with ten burgundy vinyl stools along the counter on the left side. They were still upright, mainly because they were anchored to the floor. There were about twelve small wooden tables overturned and strewn across the floor.

Everything was covered in bits of brown, amber, and

clear broken glass, and a faint whiff of old coffee grinds hung in the humid air.

The same bits of broken glass covered the floor as well, and the spiked black heel of a woman's shoe lay under one of the stools. Cheap, colorful Mardi Gras paintings hung on the walls. A couple of them were hanging at odd angles, and one lay on the floor with a broken frame. There was a TV still anchored to the wall near the ceiling. It angled downward toward the tables, although the screen had been shattered.

The old man grabbed the most intact table and set it upright, then reached down to scoop up a cheap amber glass holder with a candle in it that had managed to make it through the disaster unscathed. He set the candle and holder in the center of the table, snapped his fingers, and a surprisingly robust flame appeared. It cast just enough light to surround them all.

They each found an unbroken wooden chair, carefully brushing the vinyl cushioned seats free of dirt and glass, the debris clinking softly as it hit the floor. They set their chairs down and settled in around the table. Both women reached down and wrung the water from the bottoms of their jeans as best as they could. Kellie looked ruefully at her soaking wet shoes but decided to ignore them.

Unable to contain herself any longer, Laurie burst out, "How could you allow something like Hurricane Katrina? How? You know I'm from Louisiana, and I am so angry about it. Why? *Why?* And it's not just, 'Why did you pick New Orleans, or Houma, or Gulfport, or the different towns to devastate?' It's, 'Why do you pick *any* town to do that to?'"

<h1 style="text-align:center">CHAPTER 5</h1>

New Orleans, Louisiana

God said nothing, simply offering her his full attention.

So she went on. "Why do you pick all these families, whether it's the families from Florida last season or those in New Orleans this season? Plus I'm sure there are even more families in the future who will die! There's another huge hurricane coming again…"

"I'm well aware of how you feel about this, Laurie. I've been listening to the conversations you've been having with Kellie and others. I'm not upset, and I want to answer your questions. But I'd like you to stay calm while I do. So I'm going to give you something to keep you occupied and calm while you channel my answers. Will you play along?"

"Okay," she said, a bit warily.

"You know that model train set your son is building at home?"

Surprised, Laurie said, "Yes, but—" she broke off as a few model train cars with the partially built track and a big pile of track pieces in disarray appeared on the table.

"I'd like you to work on it here as we speak." He held

up both hands and turned all ten fingers toward himself, and four more intact tables righted themselves and slid over to bump up against the table they were sitting at, forming a nice-sized area to work on. *"He won't mind, I promise."*

Kellie noted that the candle's glow had quietly expanded to include the extra tables. With a grin, she began wiping the dirt off the surfaces with her left hand. Not bothering to hide her amusement, she watched Laurie's expressive features, seeing astonishment followed by consternation in rapid succession.

"But won't it be disrespect—" Laurie began again.

"It's not disrespectful," he interrupted. *"It will tickle me to watch you. I insist you do it. Whatever work you complete here will also appear as complete in your apartment,"* he added.

Still looking doubtful, she gave in. "Okay. Ben can always take whatever I do apart again if he doesn't like it."

"All right. Back to your 'why' questions. I know you're going to be even more ticked off when I say this, but sometimes you make me laugh."

"I make you laugh?" Laurie said incredulously, clearly offended at this remark. "I'm sure he doesn't mean he's laughing *at* you," Kellie said hastily. "I'm sure he means he's…uh…well, what *do* you mean, exactly?" She finished lamely.

"I'm laughing at some of the conversations you have with others, not at you, Laurie. There's always a reason for things—and it's not the devil. I've heard people say that to you, too, and I want you to know it's not 'the devil.' There is no 'devil.' That's a made-up concept created and perpetuated by humans. There is always a reason for every single thing that happens, and I approve each and every

one. It's all under my supervision. I know everything about all events, and I'm telling you that every one of them is meant to happen. In fact, they must *happen."*

Kellie stared at him, speechless. After a moment, she glanced at Laurie to see her reaction, and saw she was even angrier.

"You know what?" Laurie said. "I can't just sit here like I'm in church listening to the preacher and say, 'Oh, okay.' What do you *mean* they must happen? What do you mean you approved each one? *Why* must you make all these people suffer? People that trip and fall or break their legs or something, that's one thing, but you rip people's mates from their hands with rushing floodwater. Families drown as they escape into their attics, waiting for the help that never comes. You allow people to go missing.

"Shoot. We could talk about September 11th, too, while we're at it. Katrina was very much like September 11th, when people didn't know where their loved ones were.

Thousands of photographs of missing family members everywhere, so many teary-eyed people wondering: 'Is my child dead or alive? What about my dad or my mom? What happened?' It's just so, so—" Outraged, she only fumed, unable to continue.

"*You, and all humans,*" he replied calmly, "want *to have all these questions. As souls, you all come into your human lives because you* want *to be put in these predicaments.*"

Well, thought Kellie, no one could ever accuse the old man of being a people-pleaser. He did not seem to feel obligated to help them feel better, that was for sure.

Laurie found her voice again. "Guess what? I don't care how worldly our souls are. I just can't imagine my soul or any of my friends' souls saying, 'I wonder, what would it be like for the person I love the very most to just vanish and for me not to know if they are dead or alive or eaten by an alligator or what.' I really can't imagine it. I don't care how wonderful our souls may be, why would any fool or soul choose to suffer like that?"

"*It's all part of the game,*" he said.

"What game? I just want to scream right now. It's all part of the game? You know what? I disagree with you even if you are God. How can you say, 'It's part of the game'? Would I really sit up there in heaven and think to myself, 'Oh, I'm going to play the game where my heart's ripped out while I watch my child be swooshed away?' No. I don't think any soul would choose to play that game. I just don't."

"*Oh, but that's where you're wrong, Laurie. All of your souls choose to play the most horrendous games. At least from your human perspective, you see them as horrendous. From your vantage point, they seem to be the most horrible, horrible things.*

"*Listen carefully, because this is important: When you are in the spirit realm—or in heaven, however you prefer to think of it—you are in a totally different mindset. You're in a totally different space. The things that are so horrendous to your human bodies and human minds are not all that horrendous to your mighty soul. Just the way a bodybuilder would work hard to build up his muscles, your mighty, mighty, strong soul works hard to build itself up, to strengthen itself, to nourish itself.*

"*I know you're thinking, 'How could sadness be nourishing it?' But the sadness is nourishing it. The loss is completing it in a way that is hard for you humans to understand. For your soul to be totally complete, and I'm talking lifetime after lifetime after lifetime, you must experience every single thing. You must. That is why one soul takes so many different bodies, living so many different human lifetimes. There is no other way to gain that breadth of experience. It's just how the game works."*

Experience every single thing? Lifetime after lifetime? Kellie's thoughts were a whirlwind, trying to absorb the implications. But that would mean…no, it couldn't be. He was telling them that reincarnation was a reality, and that over different lifetimes, everyone would be, do and experience every—

Laurie interrupted her thoughts. "Why would you create a game with such horrible things? I'm sitting here wondering, 'Am I talking to God for real, or is this some devil spirit trying to fool me?' because I can't comprehend this. I just can't."

"It's because you don't recall what it's like to be the almighty soul, to be that all-powerful. You don't remember what it is to be tough, strong, and brave. To be able to withstand anything, to be able to hold everything."

Kellie took a deep breath. "Whoa. Let's just slow down here for a moment." She paused, pulling her thoughts together. Then she continued, speaking carefully. "Okay. So, who cares? Why do we need to do all that? Strengthen our souls or whatever. What is the ultimate point?"

CHAPTER 6

New Orleans, Louisiana

"*A*h," said the old man. "*The ultimate point is to experience every single emotion, every single thought, and every single feeling in existence. You know what? When your souls are up there—and 'there' is not really 'up'; I only use that term to make it easier to explain—your souls up there in heaven are more like when your boys were little down here. Much more like little boys than you adult women. Your almighty souls think more like: "Huh, I wonder what would hurt the most? Kellie, could you see your boys when they were younger saying, 'Would it hurt more to stick a pin in my finger or would it hurt more if you pinched it?'"*

"Well… yes," Kellie said reluctantly. "They were—still are—insatiably curious. I actually can see my boys doing that, at age three."

"*Yes, I know you can. Laurie, your son wasn't quite in that space. But Kellie, you know exactly what I'm talking about.*"

Not about to concede so easily, Kellie said, "Yes, I do. But it's because at three years old, curious little boys have no idea how much it's going to hurt when they actually *do* pinch. Then, once they do, they're sorry they did."

"*And you know what?*" he shot back. "*They'll do the very same thing the following week. It's curiosity. Your souls are very, very curious. And it's not just about which would hurt worse, a pinch or a stick. It's about, 'How would I handle the situation? How would I play the game? How would I win the game against all odds?' Life is a challenge, a challenge you choose to take on before you come into it.*"

Thinking furiously and unable to sit still, Kellie jumped up and began pacing toward the windows and back, bits of glass crunching under the heavy tread of her running shoes, still soaking wet from the watery street. "Then why are we so out of touch with that choice? Why is there not even a little piece of us that feels that curiosity or some sense of being okay with it?"

"*Because if you—not just you two but all humans on earth—were totally and completely aware, if you* knew *that, 'Oh, before I came in, I chose to go through this,' you wouldn't really* experience *it. It wouldn't be real to you. Think about it. Do you get it?*"

Kellie paused at the window, then turned around to face him, putting her hands behind her on the dirty sill and leaning back. "We wouldn't experience it as completely, as horribly, as we do. But you know, that's kind of the point. We'd rather *not* 'completely experience' every unimaginably awful detail of the really bad stuff. Or even the semi-bad stuff, for that matter. Frankly, I'm sure I could be a perfectly happy soul without having been tortured, betrayed, or dying from a horrible illness."

He rocked back in his chair, hands clasped. "*But remember, this is the soul's game. It's the soul's challenge to be able to handle these experiences, and it is also the soul's game to see* how. *'How am I going to handle this? What am I going to do?'"*

Kellie sighed. "Okay. So, when I asked you what the ultimate point was, you said the point was to experience everything, but that wasn't really my question. My *real* question is: *Why* do we want to experience everything, including all of the horrible stuff? What is the point of *that*? Are you telling me that it's just curiosity?"

"To put it pretty simply, yes, it's curiosity."

Laurie was snapping sections of train track together furiously as they spoke, and then she gave up and threw a piece down on the table. "Well, I have to tell you that, sitting up there—wherever 'there' is—being in the space of the soul, making all these decisions about what we are going to experience on a physical level, we must completely forget every time what it's like to be human. Because when you get down here and you're actually in it, no one would choose to experience these horrendous things."

"I hear what you're saying Laurie, I do. But remember, when you go through something horrible, it can give you depth of character. It can bring out parts of you that you did not even know existed before. You've been using the hurricane for an example, so let's look at that. For some people, it brought out the worst in them. It created monsters. For others, it created saints—the exact same experience. For instance, there were two brothers who lived in an area that was devastated by the hurricane. One brother chose to help a lot of his neighbors in distress. The other chose to break into a store and steal a TV.

"It's all part of the human challenge: What are you going to do? How are you going to handle something? You

get to choose how you will respond. Here's another example: Laurie, you've come in this time, in this life, to experience poverty as one of your issues. You can choose to respond by learning how to be happy without money, or, you can choose to be miserable because you have no money."

"Lovely," she said sardonically. "Well, God, I certainly hope I've already experienced that enough and I can be done with it now."

He smiled wryly. *"The part I'm not sure you're getting yet is that it's possible to choose to be happy, or at least to feel much better than you think you can, in spite of whatever your circumstances are. So here's another example: Kellie, you've come in to experience what it is like to be stuck in bed, to be bedridden. You experienced that circumstance for ten years when your illness was at its worst, which I know to you, is a long time. You had many choices on how to respond. For instance, you chose to keep searching for answers, searching non-stop for any treatments that might help you feel better or get you back on your feet. For ten years you searched and never gave up."*

"And I found a number of things that helped, and in the end I found the right doctor and treatment that got me back on my feet," Kellie finished for him.

He leaned forward and thumped his fist on the table. *"Exactly! You could have just given up and felt sorry for yourself. Lots of people in that position do. And now you have strength of character that you otherwise would not have had. That's what you wanted as a soul, to build that character, in order to work toward being fully, fully whole. That is why you chose that circumstance."*

"And what will we do with that wholeness, once we're fully whole?" Laurie demanded.

He spread his hands out, palms up. "*It takes you so, so long to get to that point and then, when you do, you'll go up there into the heavenly realm as you humans call it, and you'll stay up there and you'll, well, I'll use the word 'work,' although it's not necessarily work. You'll be up there helping others to grow and experience and learn. You'll be up there guiding humans.*"

"Really?" Kellie said, pushing off the windowsill she had been leaning on. In three long strides she was back at the table. She grabbed her chair, sat down and leaned forward eagerly. "So that's what it's all about, becoming advanced enough to be able to help others?"

He gave her a considering look. "*It's not that you get 'the big prize,' so you get to help others. It's not that you're the winner or the loser. When you're up there, you're not thinking 'Oh, I won the big prize.' When you're up there you have such a sense of well-being, such a sense of, 'Oh, this is joy. This is peace. This is total, total contentment.' And you look upon these wonderful, wonderful humans, and you simply want to help them to get to this wonderful, wonderful place where you ar*e."

He leaned forward, reaching out for a piece of train track and, choosing one with a split, locked it into place. "*You're doing a good job on this, Laurie. It's definitely keeping you calm and not nervous as we speak.*"

He sat back again and went on: "*There are not that many who have reached that complete fullness and wholeness that I'm speaking of. There are very few, in fact. But that's just because not enough time has passed. There will be more and more and more. But know this: With every single thing that you learn, with every experience that you go through,*" *there are about five million more that will make you even more complete, even more perfect, and even more satisfied."*

"So what you're saying," Kellie said, "is that it's *when* we've gone through every single experience, no matter how horrendous, that we feel that wholeness and completeness. That's how we are able to experience that joy, that wonderful, contented peace when we are done being born, living, and dying so many times that we've experienced it all, and can finally stay up there. And if we hadn't gone through it all, we wouldn't experience that kind of joy. Is that right?"

"You got it."

Kellie frowned. "Does that mean we can never experience joy or peace here on earth, right now?"

He paused for a moment. Then he said gently, *"With the knowledge I'm giving you—and I'm far from finished— you'll be able to experience more joy and peace, right here and right now, than you ever thought possible. The joy, peace, and wholeness I was just speaking of, that of a completed soul, is beyond anything you can imagine. There are simply no words in the human language to describe it. You'll just have to take my word on that."*

CHAPTER 7

New Orleans, Louisiana

"*H*ere's why you need to have every experience," the old man began. "*When you're up there, it's like watching your favorite TV program, and you have five thousand favorite TV programs.*"

He lifted his right hand and pointed to the TV on the wall with the broken screen. It made a crackling sound, and then two beeps as it suddenly lit up, the screen miraculously whole again. A montage in color of the two women and their children began to scroll across the screen, working, playing, studying, and generally going about their lives. "*One program would be called 'Laurie,' one would be called 'Kellie,' and there would be one for each of your sons: 'Aron,' 'Kyle,' and 'Ben.'—there are all these different programs.*"

He snapped his fingers, and the flowing images stopped on a frame showing Ben, Laurie's son, sitting by himself at a blue steel cafeteria table at school. There were two older boys sitting on either side of him, blocking him from getting up. A sandwich rested on a brown paper bag in front of him. One of the older boys picked it up and took a big bite out of it, laughing cruelly. They could hear the other boy taunting Ben.

The old man continued. *"So you're watching all these shows, and to be totally complete, you can't be watching Ben get picked on and think, 'Oh, I forgot to check out what it's like to have my feelings hurt.' You'll want to know exactly how it feels. That's why you'll want to experience it for yourself. There are such minute pieces to this game. You choose to learn from the different pieces as you go through your lifetimes, and your lifetimes are countless."*

Laurie bristled. "Yeah, well if I'd been there, those two boys would have learned exactly how it feels to be smacked up against the wall. I would have made sure they had *that* experience for themselves, trust me! But I get the point," she added.

Kellie looked angry on Ben's behalf as well. "I don't blame you Laurie. I'd be beyond furious if it were one of my boys. I'm furious for Ben!" She frowned. "But are all the things we want to experience unpleasant?" She leaned her elbows on the table and looked at him intently. "What about joy? What about great experiences? What about pleasure and happiness? And being rich? Do we choose to experience every single one of the wonderful things as well?"

"Of course," he assured her, snapping his fingers absently at the *TV*. The picture crackled loudly and then disappeared, displaying the broken screen once again. *"It's not that you choose only to experience and go through all of the horrible, uncomfortable experiences. You also choose experiences such as what it's like to be the most popular singer, or how it would feel to be on Forbes' number one rich gal list."*

She smiled. "So we get to experience every one of the fabulous things, too."

"Yes. But remember, the game wouldn't be the game if you did it all in one lifetime."

"Dang!" Laurie hit a curved piece of track on the edge of the table and then tossed it into the middle of the table. "I just can't find the right piece. Blasted train track!"

"That one fits perfectly, Laurie," the old man said, pointing confidently at one of the straight pieces. *"Lock it in."*

Kellie sat back in her chair, crossing her legs. "Well, I feel a lot better. Don't you, Laurie? I'm thinking of all the cool stuff we get to experience! No need to ever be envious of anyone ever again, since we all get to have what they do at some point."

"I don't know," she responded grudgingly. "It's not like we remember it from life to life. Did Kellie and I choose any of the good stuff this lifetime?"

"You never choose a lifetime to experience only the harmful, hurtful things. And you never choose a lifetime to experience only the great things. Each lifetime, you have a mixture of both. You may think some people have the perfect life, but they don't. You can name any human that you think has the perfect life, and I'll be able to tell you things about that life that are not perfect."

Laurie frowned. "I can think of people who must not ever have a single joy in their lives. What about children who are born into poverty and starve to death by the time they are two years old?"

"Yes, there are some who appear to never have joy in their lives. But it's usually in the starving communities where everything looks so bleak that the greatest love and joy comes. Because that very starving little child may have a little tiny pet and experience such love! That two-year-old might experience and express and feel more love with that pet than you experience with any lover or mate in your

entire life. Sometimes it works like that. There's always good with the bad—always, always, always. Whether you can see it or not might be a different story."

"I'd like to experience going from cash flow struggles to always having lots of cash," Kellie said. "How cool would that be?"

He smiled. *"That's very possible. You've done it before. Sometimes you choose things you've done before so you can do them again and play it a bit differently. It's not that there are set rules to this game. It's not as though every time you go from poor to rich, you do it in exactly the same way. That's part of the human choice; that's part of your free will. The game is: How are you going to act? What are you going to do with your cash? How will your personality be affected as you experience all the pressure of being wealthy?"*

"I'm ready for that challenge," Kellie declared enthusiastically.

"Yeah, well, why don't you send the cash our way first, God, and we'll let you know how it goes," Laurie said flippantly.

CHAPTER 8

New Orleans, Louisiana

"*You two must be getting hungry by now,*" the old man said, ignoring Laurie's comment. He reached under the table and pulled out two burgundy-colored menus, holding one out to each of them. Laurie took hers.

Kellie gave him a comical "Where-the-hell-did-that-come-from?" look, then bent down to peer with exaggerated astonishment under the table. She saw nothing but the flat underside. She re-emerged, squinting her eyes at him in mock suspicion this time, then snatched the menu out of his hand. "I'm still not used to this conjuring out of thin air stuff," she muttered, giving him a sidelong glance as she opened her menu. Laurie was already studying hers.

The old man just gave her a knowing smile, then surveyed the partially finished train set. He wiggled his fingers and miniature scenery began to appear around the train track. Each time something new appeared, they heard a musical chime. Each chime was a different note, so as he created, it sounded like a melody. First, bright green shrubbery and trees grew alongside the track. Then, in an explosion of red sparkles, a red station house appeared, and finally, in flashes of yellow light, blinking yellow railroad crossing signs popped up. When Kellie put down her menu, it all looked so real, she was sure the train itself would come to life and begin roaring around the track at any moment.

She eyed him speculatively. "*What?*" he said.

"I was just wondering . . . do you think you could wiggle those magic fingers of yours and conjure us up a working ladies' room?"

Laurie set her menu down. "Great idea, Kellie."

"*Of course. Go freshen up, both of you, and then we'll place our orders*." He waved his right hand casually toward the back of the café as the two women rose from their seats.

Kellie saw a door that said simply, "Toilette."

"I love the French," Laurie said wryly, leading the way. "They're so direct."

Once they returned to their seats, the old man clapped loudly once and a startled waiter appeared, arms flailing, wobbling to catch his balance. Once he had it, he stared at the yellow pencil and white order pad in his hand, as though he couldn't quite remember what they were for.

"Place your orders, ladies," the old man said absently, as he studied the winding track.

The waiter recovered himself and turned to Laurie, looking directly into her eyes and displaying an engaging grin. Around thirty-five years of age with dark skin, black hair, and Mediterranean features, he was actually quite good-looking, Kellie thought privately. He was wearing black jeans and a burgundy shirt with "Niko" embroidered on the pocket.

"I'll have the heavenly burger and a raspberry divine iced tea," Laurie said firmly.

Niko nodded, and Kellie could hear the faint scribbling of his pencil on the pad. "How would you like your burger cooked?"

"Rare, please."

He winked at her. "You got it." Laurie raised her eyebrows.

Then he turned to Kellie. "And what can I get for you?"

"I'll have the heavenly burger with cheese, medium-well, and an earth angel sangria."

He scribbled. "An earth angel sangria for the earth angel," he said flirtatiously. Kellie blushed.

He finished scribbling and turned toward the old man, who was still examining the train setup. "*I'll have the cosmic cranberry juice,*" he said.

Niko scribbled on the pad and bowed respectfully. Then he turned and winked mischievously again at the two women, walking jauntily back toward the counter. He began to fade as he moved past the edge of the candle's glow, so only the burgundy shirt was visible. Then that too slowly disintegrated into the darkness.

"You've been busy," Laurie said, nodding toward the latest additions to the train set-up. Now, the track split, with one section winding around a miniature blue lake, with six tiny white swans swimming lazily in circles. The other section wasn't built yet.

"*I love creating things,*" the old man said, his eyes glinting in amusement. "*But it's time we continued our debate. Where were we? Oh yes, Laurie wanted me to leave sacks of cash on your doorsteps, figuratively speaking, so you could play the money game. I hate to burst your bubble, but that's not going to happen. At least not for you two.*

"*I'll let you in on a little secret: The two of you already agreed to help me get this information out there to others—before you even came into this life. It's part of what you wanted to do while you were here on earth. Your personal challenges are not so different from the challenges many others face, and I intend to make sure the answers to your questions apply to everyone else as well. That means no sacks of money, and no miracle healings—at least not from me. You're going to have to learn to create the money on your own, just like everyone else."*

Laurie stiffened. "Wait just a minute. Let's go back to the 'You already agreed' part. Are you telling me we have no choice about it? We already agreed to be your messengers, so we're stuck? We have to be whether we want to or not?"

His voice softened, and he said gently, *"No, you aren't stuck being my messenger, Laurie. It's true that there are a few things that have been decided ahead of time that can't be changed—mainly because, as a soul, you didn't want to be able to change them. I'm referring to the experiences that create character we spoke about earlier. But you still have a tremendous amount of free will. You can change your mind if you want to."*

She considered. *"So, we get to have all our questions answered, and all you're asking is that we share the answers with others as well? Like, write a book or something?"*

"Sounds good to me. I'll make myself available to you at appropriate times in the future. You bring the questions, and I'll bring the answers."

"How will we know when to meet?" Laurie asked.

"Sometimes you'll just get a feeling, Laurie, and sometimes I'll speak a few words to you and let you know I'm available. Then you simply call me in the way you always call angels and guides in, and I'll either show up

where you are, where you're going, or I'll provide transport to where I want to meet you, like I did today."

The two women glanced uneasily at each other. Kellie felt a mixture of excitement about the opportunity to get the answers to *all* of her questions, and nervousness regarding the responsibility to share the answers with others. After a moment, excitement about the opportunity won. "I have goosebumps. I think I want to do this." She raised her eyebrows questioningly at Laurie, who appeared to be struggling with the decision.

Finally, Laurie shrugged. "Why not?" Kellie turned back to the old man. Taking a deep breath, she said, "Okay. We're in!"

CHAPTER 9

New Orleans, Louisiana

The old man sat back in his chair again, smiling in satisfaction. "*All right. Let's up the ante here. I'm not convinced that you completely get the whole 'game' and how it's played in your bones, so to speak. And it's critical that you, and everyone you share this information with, understands it from the get-go. So ask me some more questions, and let's get even more personal this time. And while we do, I want you to finish building the track around Swan Lake, Laurie,*" he added, pointing at the new lake on the table with the tiny swans still swimming about.

"Ooooh, he's thrown down the gauntlet, Laurie." Kellie sat up a little straighter. "You ready for this?"

"I'm ready." She began searching for pieces of curved track on the table. "But you're the personal coach; you're trained to ask good questions. Why don't you start?"

"All right." Kellie stopped to think for a moment, then snapped her fingers. "I know what I want to ask. What am I doing right now that will shorten my life or make me unhealthy later?"

He eyed her speculatively, then he said, *"You're engaging in mental sabotage and destruction."*

"What?" The shock was plain on her face.

He laughed. *"Let me put it another way: You're sunk in worry and fear. That seems to be such a common human thing. And although I created everything, I'm not going to take credit for that one."*

"You're not going to take credit for fear?" Laurie said skeptically. "Come on. I thought you created everything."

The old man pondered for a moment. *"I created every person. I dearly love every person. And yes, that includes the murderers and the ones you put the bad labels on. But not everything you read or hear about me—or what I've supposedly said—is true. Even the great ministers and preachers don't always get it right. What they say is not always directly from me either. For instance, I do not want anyone to fear me."*

Slowly recovering from her shock, Kellie pressed the issue. "You didn't invent fear?"

"Okay," he confessed. *"So I invented It, but it's being exploited, if you ask me."*

She laughed. "In other words, we're taking fear a lot farther than you intended it to go, is that it?"

"You got it. Fear was supposed to be helpful, to save your life if need be. It wasn't intended to be something that controlled your thoughts and actions much of the time."

Kellie sighed. "It's true. I worry about so many things. I guess that's really stress, right—that's what most of us would call stress?"

"You nailed it, Kellie. Stress is actually worry and fear. What I had hoped for all of you was for your automatic reaction to be happiness, love, peace, and joy.

Instead, the automatic reaction in humans seems to have become fear, fear, fear, anxiety, distress, worry, worry, upset."

"I see," Kellie said ruefully. She pointed across the table. "There's another piece of curved track on the corner there, Laurie." Looking at the old man, she asked, "Any suggestions on how I can stop worrying?"

"That's a tough one. Because as I've been explaining, life really is a game, and you're all playing it to discover the greater you, the greater gifts that you already have. You're playing it to develop those gifts, to develop yourself, and to overcome some of the things you don't care for about yourselves. That's all part of the game. But most of you judge the challenge, the difficulty, and the hard part of life as "bad"—when that is supposed to be the fun *part!"*

He waved his hand, and with a loud crackle the TV on the wall came to life again. Laurie stopped working with the track to watch. First the screen showed a large stone castle on a hill. Then it zoomed inside the castle where a group of barefoot young children in woolen clothing were running around and hiding while one hid her eyes, her lips moving as though she were counting.

The young girl hiding her eyes stopped counting and began searching, with no luck finding any of the other children, who had disappeared somewhere within the labyrinth of hallways and rooms. She clearly looked unhappy, as though she was about to cry.

He pointed at the little girl on the screen. *"Imagine you're a child playing hide and seek, and it's the part where you're 'it' and supposed to find your friends who are hiding. That's the fun part of the game. But you're not having fun. Instead of thinking 'Hmmm, where could they be? I know I can find them; how shall I figure it out?' You're stressed at having to find your friends. You're worried that you won't be able to. You're scared, thinking 'What if I never see them again?'"*

"Oh please," said Laurie, "how could it *not* have turned out like that? *Of course* real-life challenges aren't fun! They aren't fun because they're painful. They're uncomfortable. They feel bad. That's why we don't like them. Even if our 'almighty souls' want to have every experience, that doesn't mean that while we're down here on earth we're going to actually think it's *fun* to have those 'challenging' experiences!"

He sighed, and the TV went dark with a pop. *"I hear you."*

"But it sounds as though you're saying we are supposed to be able to have all of those challenges without experiencing so much suffering and pain," Laurie pressed.

"That's exactly what I'm saying."

"Okay, you wanted to make this personal," Kellie said, "so let's do it. You know I was sick and in bed for ten years with chronic fatigue immune dysfunction syndrome, or CFIDS. Ten years of my life, when most people are in their prime and fulfilling their potential, I was incredibly ill, so sick there were times in the first few years that I was crawling from my bed to the bathroom."

She shuddered, recalling those lonely, nightmarish days. Very few people had understood, because at the time there were still many who did not accept or believe the illness even existed. They thought it was psychological. Even those who accepted her condition, like her husband who supported her emotionally and physically, did not understand—not really. She swallowed, then went on. "How could that possibly have been fun? How could you reasonably expect me to think that was *fun?*" She paused, taking a moment to breathe and steady herself. Then, in an effort to keep things light, she added, "And please don't put me on TV."

"*What, you don't want to be in the spotlight?*" he joked, playing along. Then he looked serious again. "*I know you think that was very, very unfair. And a lot of things are done to help you grow and expand. Yes, I see you rolling your eyes, Laurie. Just listen.*"

He pointed at a pile of track. "*And there's another curved piece of track under that pile over there, grab it and keep building. Kellie, a lot of things happen because they are part of a bigger picture. I know you may think, 'Well, yeah, but ten years is a big chunk of life to be learning from one experience.'*

"*But consider this: that's a big chunk of your life for you to spend thirty more years growing from, and helping others who are going through something similar. You haven't even tapped into your big picture— you haven't gotten to that point yet. And you aren't supposed to. I know it's very hard to understand.*

"*You may find it interesting to know that, on a spirit level, CFIDS is a life card souls get when they have something to contribute to the world that needs to be developed mentally. The forced downtime develops their minds. So for anyone in that position, I suggest you allow ideas to come in. Ask yourself, 'Why am I in this forced downtime? What can I think about? How can I utilize this time?'*"

"I don't think she's in disagreement about the experience or what she's learned from it," Laurie stated, as she rummaged around in the pile of track, finally locating the curved piece he had mentioned. "I just think she wants you to explain to her how, under any circumstances, she could have had fun during that time—right, Kellie?"

"Yeah. Tell me God, if you had been me, running my life during those years, how would you have done it? How would you have had fun?"

"If I could have run your life during those ten years, if I was in charge as opposed to you, I would love to have had you in bed exploring, reading, and thinking, 'Oh, I don't have to do this and I don't have to do that. This is awesome. I'm here to develop my mind. I can learn about all kinds of things. I'm here to develop other parts of my life while my physical body takes a break.'

"And you may say, 'Well, why didn't you just tell me that then so I could avoid all the pain and suffering?' But you humans are supposed to figure it out for yourselves. It's your job to finally get, 'Oh, I'm supposed to do something about this.'

"Someday, a long time from now, you will be helping others who are going through the same difficulty, Kellie. I know that ten years is a long time for you, so right now, you may not think it was worth it. But in the big scheme of things, ten years is just a moment in time."

He paused, and Niko sauntered in from the darkness again, deftly lifting their burgers and drinks from a round tray. He set them down with another one of his dazzling, heart-stopping smiles. The burgers were huge. The earth angel sangria fizzed softly. Kellie took a sip and felt her mouth tingle. Colorful orange rounds, strawberry slices, and raspberries decorated all the drinks.

With a flourish, Niko then handed out long fancy silver spoons to the women. He clicked the heels of his loafers together smartly and bowed to the old man with one hand behind his back and the other held out, palm up, presenting the spoon with reverence. Then he turned, and walking backward with a thumbs-up for the women, he disappeared into the darkness once again.

The old man picked up his glass, pushed aside the fruit with the spoon, and took a long drink. Once he had set it back on the table, he said, *"You humans are very strong and very tough. You can always rebound, whether you believe it or not."*

CHAPTER 10

New Orleans, Louisiana

"I hear what you're saying," Kellie said. "Honestly, I do, and it makes sense. But frankly, I'm still not seeing the *fun* in it."

Laurie had finished the circle of track around the lake and was getting started on her burger. The old man picked up a split piece of track and snapped it into place where she had left off, so one direction went toward the lake. Then, he moved his index fingers and this time, a four-note melody rang out. A dense forest with leafy green treetops appeared in a puff of smoke on the side of track heading away from the lake. He picked up some straight pieces, reached down through the treetops, and started snapping sections of track into place, creating a straight path directly through the forest. When he was done, the trees almost completely hid the track from view.

He sat back in his chair again. "*Well, no, not everything is going to be fun all the time. When you're playing hide and seek, it's* not *always fun. Sometimes you're sitting there scratching your head thinking, 'Gosh, are they behind the tree? Are they behind the building? Which way do I go?*

I don't know which way to go.' So you're right, not every second of the game is going to be fun. Maybe I should have compared it to chess instead of hide and seek. I was using hide and seek because you two have kids who used to like to play that game."

"So what you're telling me is I really haven't seen the real reason yet for having the long illness?" Kellie asked.

"Right."

"But I will?"

"Yes. There is always a reason, a higher purpose, for everything that happens. Everything, even if you don't always know what it is at the time. And you may never know."

"I still have the illness, you know," Kellie said, idly picking the sesame seeds off her hamburger bun. "It's just not as bad. I'm sure I speak for a lot of people who have illnesses when I ask, how I can heal myself? How can I just heal myself right now and be completely healthy?"

He took a long sip from his drink, looking thoughtful. *"I'm thinking of the appropriate answer."* Finally, he said, *"What I want you to start thinking now is, 'How can I play with it?' Not 'How can I heal it?' Not 'How can I change it?' but 'How can I play with it?' You may even want to think, 'How can I trick it?' Are you following?"*

"I'm trying."

Laurie sampled her drink. "Yum," she said with approval. Then she set the drink down with a decisive thump. "Well, I'm not following. I haven't got a clue what you mean." She picked up her burger again.

He folded his hands and leaned forward, arms on the table, giving them his full attention. *"Someday, Kellie, you're going to be working with people who are going through what you're going through now. You're going to be helping them. That's how it's going to be—I'm just going to tell you that right now.*

"*So when someone comes to you and says, 'I can't get up, I can't sit up, I can't play the piano even though I used to love to play the piano,' or whatever, what are you going to tell him or her to do or not do? You're supposed to live it first so you will know what to tell others.*

"*So here's what I have to say to you today: When your body feels tired or sick, choose to go into that wonderful, happy place in your mind. I know your response is, 'I'm too tired. I can't. I can't go to the happy place.' That's a perfectly reasonable response. I know it's hard. And—I also know that you* can *do it. You just have to believe you can.*

"*Look here.*" He leaned forward and pointed at the leafy forest on the table, with the track going straight into it, then at the place where the track split. "*You can choose to take the path through the dark forest and dwell on how tired or sick you feel. Then you'll feel just as bad emotionally as you do physically.*

"*Or,*" he pointed to the split again, then at the peaceful lake with the beautiful swans swimming gracefully around, and the track curving around it. "*You can choose the other track and look for things you can do, think, and appreciate that make you feel good emotionally. Your body may still be tired or feel sick, but your state of mind will be peaceful and happy. Just because you feel bad physically doesn't mean you have to feel bad emotionally. The two are* not *mutually exclusive. In other words, you may not have control of your illness, but you do have control over whether or not you suffer from it.*"

He leaned back again in his chair. "*That's part of your*

mission at this moment, Kellie, to figure out how to get to that happy place, no matter how your body feels. I know that's not the answer you're looking for, especially from me. But that's the answer I have for you at this moment in time. And remember, I don't just throw out things for no reason. People don't get diseases for no reason. Tell that to your friends. More importantly, tell it to the world.

"I'm not going to say you're not going to be healed if you don't do this, but you will be healed and feel better sooner *when you get yourself into that pleasant, happy state of mind. And no, you're not sitting in a pile of daisies. That isn't what your soul wants for you right now."*

Kellie picked up her earth angel sangria, using the opportunity to absorb the information he'd just given her. She realized she was very thirsty and promptly drained half the glass. After setting it back down, her mouth and throat tingling, she said, "I'm going to have to let that sink in. I really don't have any more questions right now. Laurie, are you ready for your turn? I'm more than happy to give up the hot seat for a while and demolish this burger," she said, eyeing it hungrily.

"Lovely. I'm so looking forward to this," Laurie said sardonically. "But yeah, I'm ready."

She quickly polished off the last bite of her burger and then began: "I'm not having fun. Everything is a job; everything is a hassle. I'm just overwhelmed all the time. I have so many projects that need my attention, I just want to hide under the covers and sleep all day. My friends are too demanding, they want to talk on the phone all the time and I feel drained by it. Quite obviously, I haven't figured out how to play my own game properly.

"I would love to do whatever my purpose in life is,

whatever my job should truly be. But between my diabetes and my hectic schedule, I feel like I don't even have any energy left to do anything. How can I get anything done, how can I help more people more effectively, and not want to be sleeping all the time?"

The old man pointed at the forest, where the track ended. *"Keep working on the track, Laurie. This is when it's important, when you're in the hot seat. Now, with regard to your question, why don't you just do what you tell everybody else to do? Do something nice for yourself,"* he said reasonably. *"If you would take a few minutes and say, 'These are my thirty minutes for myself,' I mean, consciously say* it, *and don't fall asleep through it, and* enjoy *it, you're going to have triple the energy. Thirty minutes is all you need. Can you do that?"*

She stood so she could reach down through the treetops of the forest and continue the straight line of track. Methodically snapping pieces together, she said, "It sounds easy. But clearly I haven't been able to do it yet."

"When you do, you'll have much more energy. Just like Kellie—it's your mental *state of mind that's going to make the biggest difference. I want you both to listen and hear this again: It's your* mental *state that's going to make the difference in how you feel and in your health more than anything else. Kellie, are you listening?"*

"I'm all ears."

"Humans are always looking for the great therapist, the great antidepressant, the great holiday, the great whatever. That's not the jackpot. That's not going to do it for you. Here's what will: Take a few moments to be 'on holiday' and relax every single day."

CHAPTER 11

New Orleans, Louisiana

"*Take a few moments to just smile and be happy and appreciate what's around you, even if you don't care for what's around you,*" the old man continued. "*There's* always *something good in every single thing.*"

"In other words," Kellie said, "instead of focusing on what we *don't* like, even if we don't like a whole lot, you want us to look for and find things we *do* like and appreciate them."

He nodded. "*That's right.*"

"I'd love to hear a specific example regarding Laurie's life. Earlier, you talked about how you would have run my life when I was sick. If you were Laurie, and were running her life right now, what would you do?" Kellie asked.

He smiled. "*I would wake up, stretch, and remind myself how lucky I am to have so many different projects going on and so many different people wanting to work with me. I'd marvel at the fact they were all good partners, every one of them. I'd reflect on how lucky I was to have such a loving son and so many friends that want to speak with me. I'd get up and go get my coffee, feeling overjoyed, happy, and thankful for all of those things."*

Both women stared at him. A piece of track hung motionless, dangling from Laurie's fingertips.

"Dang, that was a really good example," Kellie said. "What a different way of looking at it!"

"And I would not be eating sugar and chocolate all the time, then compensating for it with insulin like you do, Laurie," he added. *"As a special treat, maybe. But as a diabetic, I would take better care of my body in general."*

"Now wait just a minute," Laurie began, pointing the track in her hand at him. But Kellie jumped in quickly to head her off. She said soothingly, "I imagine it's pretty tough to just stop eating sugar, especially if all you have to do is add insulin to balance your blood sugar. Look at all the people out there who want to lose weight and struggle with sugar and with carbs—which turn to sugar in our bodies. I think the real question we want answered is, what can we do to make our challenges easier? Besides just looking at them differently? Do you understand what we're asking?"

He reached out, picked up several pieces of straight track, and began handing them to Laurie, motioning her to snap in more pieces. *"I understand perfectly. You're asking me what you can do so you don't truly experience the very thing that, as a soul, you came here to experience."*

"That's not what she said!" Laurie protested.

"I know. I'm putting it like that so you both take another look at the question."

"We don't want to experience the difficult things so deeply," Laurie said. "We want it to not be as horrible, and there are lots of people who have it even worse than we do. I'm sure they'd like to have their challenges be not as bad.

But, what you're telling us is that our souls wanted it to be every bit as bad as it is. Are you telling us we're supposed to be learning some lesson or some—"

He sighed in exasperation, dropped the tracks in his hand onto the table with a clatter, put his elbows on the table, and dropped his head down in his hands. "*No. No. No. No. No. It's not that you're being sent here to learn lessons, lessons, and more lessons. You're being sent here to decide, 'How am I going to play this game?' You don't have to learn a lesson every day.*"

He looked up at them again, dropping his hands. "*Before you come into this life, you choose certain experiences you want to have. It's like when you begin a card game, you might start out with a hand of five cards. One card could be, 'You'll have a child who dies,' another might be, 'You'll be a successful, popular actor,' another might be, 'You'll be seriously injured in a car accident.' One might even be, 'You'll come into a windfall of money.' You have a lot of choices and free will as to how you play your cards, and how you play the game in general. But those cards are your hand. They form the basis of your game. They won't change. If they did, your soul wouldn't be happy. Because that larger part of you wouldn't get a chance to develop the way it desires to. I know I'm harping on this, but it's all about how you play your cards. That's it. End of story.*"

Stubbornly persistent, Kellie said, "Is there any way *at all* to play our cards so we get the most satisfying or the best result, yet experience the painfulness of it as little as possible?"

He leaned back, eyeing her and nodding slightly. "*I see. You want to know how to play the game so you don't get the full experience your soul wants.*" His eyes twinkled mischievously. *"I'm playing with you right now. I'm hoping you're getting this. I'm having a good time with it. I don't know if you are, but I am."*

"We're still resisting it," Kellie said.

"Yeah. You are. Laurie, I can see you getting worked up again. I want you to fix this part of the track to keep you calm." He pointed at a section. *"See how that piece is too big, and that one is too small? Change it around."*

She studied the track where he was pointing. "I see." She disconnected a piece of poorly fitting track. "All right. I get your point on how it doesn't make sense to *not* experience things the way we ourselves chose to as a soul and all that. But I'm still going back to the hurricane survivors, especially the survivors who lost their families, the ones who survived when the rest of their families didn't. The ones who had to watch their loved ones drown and suffer. Why do it so harshly? It's so awful."

She finished fixing the section and stood up straight again, facing him squarely. "First, those people got to experience love of their family. But then they had to experience the loss of a family member or members, loss of their pets, *and* loss of their—oh, yeah—every damned thing they ever dreamed of having? Everything they spent their whole lives building? Every memory, every photograph, every piece of clothing, every single thing, just ripped from them, literally washed away with the water?"

She put her hands on her hips. "Did they really have to go through such a horrible, horrible event? Couldn't they have experienced loss in a little lesser way, in not such a harsh way, or not all at the same time?"

The old man didn't respond immediately. Instead, he wiggled his fingers, and a small village of tiny houses sprang up, several with little smokestacks sporting wispy plumes of gray smoke snaking thinly into the air. Then he spoke. *"I'm going to keep bringing you back to the perspective of your soul, because that's what you're just not getting. One lifetime, you'll choose a card: 'What's it like to have my mate swept from my hands? What would it be like? Ooooh . . . what would it be like? How could I handle it? How would I play if every single thing was taken from me? How would I play then?' I don't know how else to explain it to you two."*

"I get it," Kellie said reluctantly. "What you're saying is that, before they came into this life, they decided they *wanted* to experience 'every single damned thing' being lost. If it were less than that, it wouldn't be the experience they wanted."

Laurie snorted. "Yeah. Can you see us writing this in a book and distributing it to all of the hurricane survivors? They'd stone us. 'Hey, you chose this as a soul before you came into this life. You wanted it.' I do not see *that* being a popular book."

CHAPTER 12

New Orleans, Louisiana

"*Are you looking to be popular, or are you looking to spread the truth?*" the old man asked pointedly.

"Well, I'd kind of like to do both," Laurie said defiantly. She began laying track around the houses he had just added.

Kellie spoke in what she hoped was a reasonable voice. "You can't spread the truth without being popular. Because if you're not popular, no one listens. No one buys the book. It is a dilemma, isn't it? 'Hey, everyone, here's a book with the answers, even if you don't like them.'"

Unconcerned, he said, "*Yep. That's it. It's up to you guys. You two can figure that part out.*"

"Right, Kellie. We'll just figure it all out; it'll be a piece of cake," Laurie said, her voice laced with cynicism. She finished laying down the final piece of track so it all flowed together in unbroken loops around the tables, pounding it with her fist to snap it into place a little harder than necessary.

"I don't understand why you want us to put this information out there," Kellie said. "If we can't make things any better, if we can't change our cards and we're all just having the experiences our souls have chosen, what difference does it make? Why bother explaining it? What is the point?"

He surveyed the finished track winding around all of his miniature creations. He nodded slightly, snapped his fingers, and the small train cars waiting on the edge of the table vanished. Then, they heard a tiny chug-chug-chug, and out of the shiny red train station the cars emerged one at a time, led by a black engine with little puffs of black smoke coming out of the tiny stack. It headed toward the first pair of blinking yellow railroad lights, which began making the universal "clang-clang" crossing bell warning sounds. The two women watched the lifelike train in wonder. As it approached the crossing, the engine emitted a long, deep, low sound from its impossibly tiny horn.

As they watched and listened, enthralled, he spoke quietly. *"What is the point? You two, in the past five minutes, have thought about life in a completely different way. Don't tell me you haven't. Kellie?"*

She tore herself away from the train set and looked at him reluctantly. "Well, you sort of forced us to."

"Laurie?"

"Yeah. I'll admit it. Yeah. But I'm not sure it's helped us."

Without warning, he stood up and flung his arms wide. The entire train set-up disappeared. In a flash of brilliance, the interior of the bar exploded into beautiful white light. A thundering sound filled their ears, as though they were standing next to a waterfall. The old man appeared to be the source of both. Kellie felt an overwhelming sense of peace, as though she was being held in the strongest of arms and the gentlest of embraces at the same time. He seemed . . .

more, somehow, though he also seemed the same. They gaped at him.

The roaring waterfall died down, and his voice took on a deep, resonating timbre, echoing faintly somewhere off the walls, which had vanished from sight in the presence of the full-bodied, rich white light.

"I'm not saying you agree with me. I can see the two of you aren't jumping up and down shouting, 'Yay. Go, team!' What I'm saying is that you both began to look at life *in a little different way, and that you will help others to do the same. Now, of course, you get to talk directly to me. I can make sure the shift happens a bit faster and you two are easy to explain things to, whereas a lot of other people are not. And you know what? That's their choice, to be stubborn.*

"It's one of the cards they chose a long time ago. 'I'm going to be stubborn in this lifetime.' Or maybe they chose the opposite card. 'You know what? I am going to try being kind of a pushover in this lifetime.' There are so many cards and so many games to play as you go back and forth, back and forth, into different lifetimes and situations. Back and forth from heaven to the earthly plane."

"I want you two to help others think, 'Huh. Maybe there's a little different way of looking at things. Maybe there is a little different way of handling them. Maybe how I handle things is what life is actually about. Maybe that is life. *Maybe there is destiny out there, and maybe I can alter it.*

"'Maybe I can have a destiny to be rich, and when I'm rich, I can be greedy and hoard all the money, or gamble it away, or drink it away. Or maybe I can be rich in exactly the way destiny has it planned: I can be generous, I can be loving, I can be giving, and I can enjoy it and have my

family enjoy it. I can help all the starving children.' There are always pieces to your destiny that are set and there are pieces that can be altered.

"This interaction we are having right now is intended to help you and everyone who receives this message know that the whole game of life is simply this: 'Am I going to choose to play the game this way or that way? Which way?' That's all there is to it. 'How am I going to play my personal game? What decisions am I going to make? How am I going to play the cards I'm dealt?'"

"And, just as soon as you start looking at your lives that way," he paused and looked pointedly at each of them in turn, *"then the game will become much more interesting. And you know what?"* His voice softened. *"The things you call horrible, no, they're not going to end."* He shook his head. *"Nope. They're not. They're just not. It's how you deal with them, how you handle them—that's what can change. That's what can make you live a happy life or live a miserable life. It's not the circumstances. It's you. It's how you handle those circumstances, that's where the difference comes in. Do you get it now?"*

"I get it now," Kellie said.

"I still don't like it," Laurie said, "but I get it."

He clapped his hands, and they found themselves standing back in Laurie's living room. The entire train setup was spread out on the living room floor, still beautiful, although rather than real water and living swans, the scenery was now crafted in lovely, but ordinary, ceramic and wood.

The old man was gone, but his last words hung vibrantly in the air: *"And there you have the game."*

PART II

THE CREATING GAME

CHAPTER 13

Central Park, New York City, New York

"So, have you given any more thought to working for the US government?" Kellie asked casually. In comfortable sweatshirts, blue jeans, and sneakers, she and Laurie were strolling in Central Park a couple of days after the discussion with God in New Orleans. It was a brisk, somewhat breezy day, but the sun was out. The two women had done their coaching and psychic calls in the morning and had the afternoon free. The pleasant sound of children playing mingled with the faint sounds of traffic. Somewhere nearby, a radio softly played the latest top pop hits.

"Actually, I have," Laurie said calmly. "It's so hard to describe how I feel about it. On one hand, it's the biggest thrill around: exciting, daring, dangerous, and adventurous. I love the heady feeling of power I get when I'm doing that work and making a huge difference in the world, saving so many lives. On the other hand, my son means the world to me. He's everything, and I never, ever want to put him in danger of any kind. And that work *is* dangerous. If the wrong people knew I was doing it . . ." she let her voice trail off.

"I get it," Kellie said. "At least, from the outside looking in, it certainly seems exciting and dangerous. And what I really get the most is you not wanting to put your son in danger. I certainly would feel that way about my boys."

"Yeah." Laurie said, sighing in disappointment. "So I'm going to call her tomorrow and tell her no."

"You made the right decision," Kellie said comfortingly.

Laurie nodded glumly. They walked in silence for a short while, then she said, "Let's change the subject. I don't know if you ever saw 101 Dalmatians, but there's a part in the beginning where the people looked just like the dogs they were walking." As she spoke, she covertly pointed out a short, rotund woman with small eyes and big fluffy auburn hair. The woman was walking a red Chow-Chow. Both she and her dog appeared to have identical expressions of aloofness on their faces, as though it were a concession to walk amongst the common folk. "I think it's true. I think a lot of people really do look the same as their dogs, don't you?"

"Yeah," Kellie said, chuckling. "Look over there!" She nodded toward another pair—a man with a long thin face, short dark brown hair, big brown eyes, and long, lanky legs. He was walking a Doberman Pinscher.

"Seems as though 'like' really does attract 'like' a lot of the time," Laurie said. "Sometimes I see it with people as well, like that couple over there." Angling herself in their direction so Kellie could see, she paused to wait for her reaction.

Kellie laughed. "You mean that couple holding hands over there? The pair who look like Tom Cruise and Katie Holmes?"

"They're the ones."

Kellie squinted one eye at them, considering. "Okay, I see your point."

Laurie stopped suddenly. "This feels like the right spot. The message I got earlier from God was that I'd know where to stop, and I'm getting that this is the place."

Kellie looked around, and then pointed. "There's a nice patch of grass. We can sit down while you call him in."

"Looks good to me." They sat down, crossing their legs. Laurie closed her eyes. "The air feels expansive here." She took a deep breath. Folding her hands in her lap, she visibly relaxed. "I'm encircling the two of us with beautiful white light . . . I'm sensing the light moving in a figure eight all around us, kind of like a soft breeze. Hmm . . . Okay, Kellie's guides, come on in and give me a signal . . . My guides, hold the space . . . They're all here . . ." She squared her shoulders a bit. "All right, here we go: Yo, God!"

"Hey," Kellie said suddenly. "That man who just walked up and began chatting with the Tom and Katie look-alikes seems familiar! Isn't that—"

Laurie opened her eyes, then rolled them toward the sky. "I could have just skipped the whole set up. He was already here!"

Kellie looked doubtful as she rose to her feet. "I'm not so sure about that. I didn't notice him until *after* you were done."

Laurie shrugged and stood up as well, brushing some loose grass off her jeans.

Just then, the man glanced their way, turned back to the couple and said something, then turned again and began walking toward them. He was dressed in the style of one of Central Park's horse-and-carriage drivers: black pants, white shirt with a khaki vest, and a high black top hat. He approached them, tipping his hat politely as he stopped.

"Where's your carriage?" Kellie asked curiously as

she looked past him, searching the area where he'd been standing.

"*Right over there,*" he nodded.

They turned around, and Kellie gasped. She could have sworn the beautiful red and white carriage and white horse had not been there a moment earlier. Under her breath so only Laurie could hear, she said, "At least he doesn't look like his horse."

Laurie laughed out loud and then quickly covered her mouth with her hand.

"*We won't always meet this often,*" he began, "*but since Kellie is here for a short time visiting, we're going to make the most of it.*" He continued coolly: "*I'm aware of your previous conversation. In fact, it suggests a topic I think is important for us to discuss, before we get into some of your other questions about life, love, happiness, and all that jazz.*"

"What's that?" Laurie asked warily.

Instead of answering her, he said, "*Come meet Seraphina. She loves meeting new people.*" They walked over to greet the lovely horse, and Kellie put her hand out to be sniffed. She adored animals of all kinds and had a habit of rescuing strays, then finding them homes, even if the home happened to be hers.

She ran her hand along Seraphina's faintly shimmering white neck. She felt a gentle tingle in her palm as her hand continued up and along the horse's broad, warm back. There were no reins or halter of any kind that she could see. Moving in front of the horse, she looked into Seraphina's gentle, loving eyes and could have sworn they were brimming with humor and intelligence. Stroking the velvety-soft nose, she suddenly felt a marvelous sense of well-being, and she gave the horse a contented smile.

The old man smiled as well, appearing pleased at her reaction. *"Let's take a ride, shall we?"*

"With pleasure," Kellie said, and as they climbed up into the carriage, he lifted each of them by the hand, escorting them onto the red velvet bench seat as though they were the finest of royalty. He walked around to the other side and stepped up gracefully, sitting to the left of Laurie, who was seated in the middle.

Without any overt signal, the horse began to move forward. Kellie looked around at the beautiful scenery, enjoying the ride and the pleasant breeze ruffling her hair. It was more noticeable up in the carriage. It wasn't so far into autumn that the leaves had changed color. Brown trunks rose high in the air, topped with leafy green crowns. Grass spread everywhere, except for the asphalt roadway they traveled on and the concrete walkways snaking around the park. A squirrel jumped from one tree to the next. Laurie kept her eyes on the old man, waiting a bit tensely for him to continue.

"This session today is very important," he began. *"You need to understand this concept I'm going to teach you, because it's like a computer program that runs in the background of all the personal life games you're playing.*

"If you imagine that the game on the computer is similar to the game you're playing in life, and that there's a hidden program running in the background that influences the way your game goes, you can see why it's important to know something about that hidden program."

He leaned to the right toward them, speaking in a confidential tone as though he were sharing a valuable secret. *"In fact, if you understand how it works, you can actually* use *the program to enhance and support your game."*

He sat back up again. *"On the other hand, if you* don't *understand what it does or how it works, it can actually sabotage your game without your knowing, or at least make it much harder. Are you following me?"*

"So far, so good," Kellie said cheerfully. The beautiful day and the stroll in Central Park had put her in a splendid mood.

Laurie ticked off the four fingers on her left hand, one by one: "One: personal life game; two: program that runs in the background and influences that game; three: I can influence that program to help make my life better; and four: I can also ignore it, in which case it might make my life worse. Got it," she said.

"Good," he said. *"Let's begin at the most basic level: Everything in existence actually vibrates at a level so fine it can't be seen by the human eye or be measured by any instruments you currently have. Your science has not evolved to the point yet where you understand that, but scientists will eventually be able to prove it. In the meantime, you'll have to take my word for it.*

"I'm going to ask you to stretch your imaginations even further. I'd like you to consider that there are things you can't see that have that vibration as well." He tapped his index finger on the side of his head. *"For example, your thoughts. Believe it or not, your thoughts also have a very fine vibration. Yes, I know, you don't think that thoughts are real enough to have a vibration at all. But they are, and they do. Eventually your scientists will figure that out as well. This is actually a very advanced scientific fact."*

He held both of his hands out in front of him, palms upward.

"So let's jump to, 'Like attracts like.'" With each "like,"

he raised first his left palm, then his right. "*It goes way beyond people looking like their dogs or couples looking like each other. It's true in more ways than you may realize. Everything that* is, *including your thoughts, vibrates. So if you want something that* is, *then if you have thoughts that have the same vibration as the thing you want, guess what?*" He moved his hands together until they clasped in front of him.

"Like attracts like?" Kellie guessed. "So that thing will come closer to you, because things, or thoughts, that vibrate in the same rhythm, just kind of naturally move toward each other?"

"*That's correct.*"

"So if you think happy thoughts, you'll attract happy things, and if you think gloomy thoughts, you'll attract gloomy things," Kellie said

"*Yes.*"

She snapped her fingers. "It's similar to what you told us at the café about playing the game, just presented a bit differently. For instance, you asked us to look at our life and our challenges differently, in a more positive and productive way. To see the positive side and the opportunities, instead of the negative side. Except it wasn't to attract what we wanted, but just to feel better, happier, and have more fun. Now, you're saying it will also help us bring more of what we want to us, right?"

He nodded again. "*Yes. Let's call it, "The Creating Game. You are able to create what you want by choosing thoughts that are similar in vibration to the things you want: the vibration that you can't prove exists—yet—but I'm telling you it does.*"

"I can imagine feeling better if I look at things a bit differently, but I'm not sure I buy the rest of it," Laurie said flatly.

CHAPTER 14

Central Park, New York City, New York

Kellie rolled her eyes. "Oh, boy, here we go."

He shrugged. *"You don't have to buy it, Laurie. But I'm curious: What's your objection?"*

She looked at him skeptically. "C'mon! If this 'Creating Game' really worked, then everyone would have everything they wanted. And we know that's not the case!"

"I said it was a program that ran in the background *and could* influence your game one way or the other. I didn't say it controlled the *whole* game. Remember, everyone has a handful of life cards they started out with. Besides, how many people do you know who are actually able to play the Creating Game consistently?"*

"Probably not many," she admitted. "Still, I know a whole lot of people who've been asking for, wishing for, praying for things for years: promotions, more money, a life partner to help raise their kids, or even just to get out of debt or be able to pay their bills on time—and they still don't have them. You'd think some of them would be good at it. So, what's up with that?"

He turned to face them. Meanwhile, Seraphina kept

walking at the same pace, her feet rhythmically hitting the hard pavement with a steady clip-clop, clip-clop. *"There's a lot more to the Creating Game than just sitting there meditating or saying you want something. You think the Universe will give it to you, but there are ten more steps to it than you realize. For instance, do you think you deserve it?"*

"Of course I do," Laurie said promptly.

"Really?" He leaned over and put his index finger on Laurie's heart. *"I'll tell you right now, in your heart of hearts, ninety-nine percent of you humans think you* don't *deserve it, whether you admit it or not."*

He sat up straight and looked forward again. *"Then there are all of those blocks you have to achieving your desires. I could write a book—oh wait, I am writing a book, or you are for me."*

He grinned. *"For example, many of you have a desire to be healthier, but you wouldn't know what to do with yourselves if you weren't complaining about your headaches or tiredness. There's a lot more internal work than you realize that needs to be done first."*

They began to pass a row of large trees on their left, with glimmers of sunlight filtering through the leaves here and there. The old man waved his hand casually at the treetops. They looked up, and images began to form in the leaves. Kellie blinked, unsure if she was seeing things or not. But the images were still there, carved from the leaves: cars, people holding hands, houses, executive office buildings, stacks of cash, and more.

He continued. *"You need to feel that you're ready, that you're up to it, that you deserve that new job, car, or relationship. Are you prepared for the love of your life? Can you actually handle sharing your space with someone else right now? You'd all love to win a million dollars, but are you ready to deal with everyone you know or meet wanting a piece of it? What will you do with it? Are you ready for the responsibility? There's so much more depth and complication to it than you realize."*

"That's a neat trick," Laurie commented. The pictures in the treetops had caught her eye and she was entranced. Tearing her gaze away and looking at him, she asked, "So, how do we know if we're ready?"

"Ask yourself the hard questions. For instance, instead of simply saying 'I want to be in the perfect relationship,' ask yourself: 'Do I really want to share a bathroom every day? Do I really want to have sex? Do I really want to check in regularly so someone else doesn't worry about me?'"

Laurie laughed. "Do I really want to have sex? Who doesn't want to have sex?" He raised an eyebrow at her. *"You'd be surprised."*

He waved his hand at the treetops again and the pictures melted, disappearing into the leaves. *"Then, you have to consider that you're not supposed to have everything you want. Remember the cards you get at the beginning of the game? A lot of times your path is to teach you to dig deep into your soul. It's to learn how to make it when you don't have enough money. It's to discover that you can be independent without a mate to lean on. In other words, sometimes the life experiences your soul has chosen are contrary to your human desires."*

The ride became bumpy as the carriage rolled over some gravel in the roadway. Kellie's voice came out a little jerky, and she spoke loudly to be heard over the gritty sound of the crunching wheels. "In other words, sometimes the hand of cards you get for your life game stops your desires from manifesting, so you can play the way your soul wants."

"You're catching on," he said approvingly. *"I'd also like to mention that so many humans are angry with me because I don't give them what they want. They don't understand that it's not all about me granting wishes to people like birthday wishes or a genie in a bottle. Universal law plays a significant role. It's The Creating Game. 'Like attracts like.' It's that simple."*

The ride smoothed out again. *"I will help things along if you ask me to, but unless it's one of your cards and part of your game, it's not a good idea for me to help you to get that bartending job if you have the tendency to be an alcoholic. That goes double for relationships. The relationships people* think *they want are, more often than not, bad for them. I wouldn't be doing any favors by helping facilitate those relationships. Sometimes it's a wonderful gift when a relationship doesn't work out."*

"Yeah, I've had so many relationships I've wanted that didn't work out, you must have been working overtime to *not* help me," Kellie said dryly. "But I have to admit, with every one, in the long run I was thankful it didn't."

Her legs were beginning to cramp a bit from being in the carriage, so she stretched them out. She leaned over to massage the muscles of her calves to buy time, thinking of where she wanted to go next with her questions. She made up her mind and sat up. "You said you'd help if we asked. So just to clarify, that means that, in addition to us playing the Creating Game, you'll give things a push in the right direction for us as well, as long as it doesn't interfere with our life game?"

"Yes, on anything you need help on. And just having the thought to call me in and to say, 'Hey, God, help me lose weight,' or, 'Hey, help me eat properly,' will put you in the

right frame of mind to attract it. But you need to know that unless you ask me to, I'm not going to come in and help," he added. *"Most of the time I don't mess with your game unless I have your permission."*

"So basically, you're telling us to pray," Kellie said matter-of-factly. *"Basically, I am,"* he agreed. *"It doesn't have to be a formal thing in church or kneeling with your hands folded. You can be washing the dishes or riding a bike. Just think 'Yo, God,' and I'll hear you."*

"So we don't have to stand on ceremony."

"Not at all. But don't get me wrong: There's nothing wrong with ceremony either. That can actually help some people focus their thoughts in the right direction."

A very large green grassy area appeared on their left, dotted with people picnicking on blankets, tossing Frisbees, playing catch with baseballs, chasing young children, and generally having a relaxing day in the breezy sunshine at the park. A man was playing a string guitar, the gentle melody wafting on the breeze. One boy was attempting to get a yellow kite down from the tree it was stuck in. The old man waved his hand, and the kite suddenly detached, tumbling and dipping in the air as it sailed down onto the grass.

The boy ran over to the kite where it lay on the ground. Kellie gave the old man a thumbs up and continued. "Okay. I have another question. You offered 'Help me lose weight,' as one of your examples. Many people who consider themselves experts in positive thinking—in the Creating Game—say you have to act and speak as though you already have what you want, as I mentioned earlier. For instance, you might say, 'I'm exactly the weight I want to be,' and imagine that you already are. But you don't seem to be emphasizing that. Why not?"

He shook his head. "*It's not necessarily true that you must speak and act as though you already have what you want. If you can do it, that's great! But it's just not realistic for many people who can't even drag themselves out of bed, for instance, to say to themselves, 'I have energy.' They really don't feel it and it's not going to be effective. A more realistic happy medium would be, 'I'm creating energy—I feel more energetic today than yesterday,' something like that. That will get you on the right road, and it won't feel like it's impossible. And when you ask me for help, asking for 'more energy' is just fine.*"

"As long as we believe it's possible," Kellie said.

"*Yes.*"

She relaxed back into the carriage seat. "Well, that certainly sounds much easier!"

CHAPTER 15

Central Park, New York City, New York

As they came to the end of the grassy area, they saw the vendor at a hot dog stand put three juicy-looking hot dogs into steaming buns and hand them out to a man and his two young children. "Oh, that looks good!" Kellie said. "Can we stop? Do you want one Laurie?"

The old man whistled, and Seraphina stopped. "Sure, why not?" Laurie said. They jumped down from the carriage. Kellie looked at him inquiringly, and he waved her on. "*Go ahead, I'll wait here.*"

They walked over to the cart. Kellie's stomach rumbled, reminding her how long it had been since breakfast. Returning with two large hot dogs, they stood by the carriage eating, mustard oozing out from the end of the buns. The old man swung out of the carriage seat and went up to Seraphina's head, offering her an apple he pulled from behind his back. She took the apple gently into her mouth and began crunching delicately.

Kellie finished her dog first. "So, don't you think finding a happy medium seems easier, Laurie? Finding a way to look at something that's more positive, but still realistic?"

Laurie shrugged. She popped the last bite into her mouth and wiped her hands on the clean part of the napkin. "That makes it sound a *little* easier, but still, it seems as though there are so many reasons we might not be able to attract what we want, there isn't much point in even trying."

"*Of course there is.*" The old man came around the side of the carriage and offered his hand to each of them in turn, gallantly assisting them back up into the seat.

"*As long as you're not trying to attract the wrong things—things that go against what your soul wants, or things that aren't good for you and you'd be better off without. You won't get those.*"

He slid into the seat beside them, spreading both arms on the back of the carriage seat. Seraphina began moving forward again. "*But you can have many, many things you want. For instance, you can attract the health you want as long as you do your part and meet the Universe halfway. Even if one of your cards is to have the experience of a horrible disease, you can certainly recover—unless it's your time to die. Death has its own set of rules,*" he added. "*We'll talk more about that later on.*"

"What do you mean 'If you meet the Universe halfway?'" Kellie asked.

He sighed. "*I mean, you can't just sit on your butt watching TV and eating Oreos all day, saying 'I want a million dollars, I want a million dollars,' or even 'I have a million dollars, I have a million dollars,' and expect to attract it—unless having that kind of money is just one of your soul cards this lifetime. I think I'll call them 'soul cards' from now on. But most people, including you two, don't happen to have that card. So, you must be out there working hard, doing whatever it takes to earn that money.*"

That shows you're serious about it. Your intention is clear. Just by working toward it, your focus and attention on it will help bring it to you."

The carriage stopped and he nodded toward the right. *"That's the Manhattan Upper East Side over there. Most of those people chose or attracted 'old money' and their game is how to manage all the challenges that come with old money."*

He then nodded toward the left. *"That's Manhattan's Upper West Side. Those people chose or attracted 'new money' and their game is managing everything that comes with that. Guess what game they play in Harlem?"*

Before either of them could answer, he grinned. *"The neighborhood's been changing recently, but for a long time, they attracted 'no money,' so their game was to figure out how to manage that."*

Seraphina began moving forward once again. *"Let's get personal,"* he went on. *"Laurie, you get such delight in telling people how much stuff you get for free. You're quite proud of getting the best discounts and deals. You love finding things on sale. You don't even realize the pride you have in getting things for a bargain or for free. If you had a ton of money, you'd still go to Target and look for sales, because it's fun for you! That's your money game."*

"I do love a bargain," she admitted.

"Both of you have been struggling with cash flow for years, and yet part of both of your games was to learn how to create money. Kellie, you've been supporting your family for a while now. You've done a great job—and you have a lot more confidence in yourself. That's significant. From your soul's point of view, that was a big success."

He raised his eyebrows and looked at them with

amusement from under his high-top hat. He pointed at first Kellie, then Laurie. *"Both of you can create cash out of thin air, even though you say you can't. But I've seen you do it."*

His tone shifted from amusement to soft and sympathetic. *"I know it's tough, when you feel as though you don't have money or health, to try and feel as though you do, so you can attract it. You both know those games all too well. And, when you can get yourself to step up to the plate, when you can walk around feeling abundant, or at least as though you are on your way, you* will *attract abundance of all kinds, including financial."*

He held both of his arms wide for a few moments. *"The more difficult games get much bigger prizes, just like at the fair. When people have money, they get more of it, because like attracts like. When you feel bad, you attract more of that. Wealth isn't necessarily green paper in your hand, either. It might be that you have a roof over your head, a car to drive, and clothes to wear."*

They were approaching a section of roadway that looked down on the right side over a lovely fountain below. There was a statue of an angel on top of the fountain, with sparkling water trickling down to a round pond beneath. On the edge of the water sat the festive Boathouse restaurant, where patrons could watch the people paddling canoes around on the glassy lake. Seraphina stopped once again. They gazed out at the beautiful scene, captivated by its charm.

"That is the very center of Manhattan," he said. *"Don't you think it's appropriate that there's an angel at the center? That's not an accident, you know."*

"It's beautiful," Kellie said softly. Laurie nodded in agreement.

After a while, Seraphina started walking again, and the wheels began to creak softly as they rolled past the fountain.

Laurie frowned. "I'm still feeling a bit lost about when it doesn't work. About when you think you're doing everything right, when you do act and think and feel upbeat and positive, and it still doesn't seem to happen. I know you've mentioned some reasons, but can you say more about the obstacles inside of us that keep us from being able to create what we want?"

He took off his top hat and set it on his lap, pausing while he considered. *"Well, there are a number of reasons it might happen, and it's different for every person. Many people are so used to having the same limiting beliefs and thinking the same thoughts as a result, they don't even realize it. Some examples are, 'I always have just enough to get by,' 'there's never enough,' 'cancer is almost impossible to beat,' 'I don't deserve it,' and 'I'm not worthy enough for it,' to name a few of the most common.*

"It takes a lot of work to get rid of the beliefs that are blocking you. Most people are totally unaware that they even have them. Limiting beliefs are often learned in childhood. Sometimes they are so strong, they even carry over from past lives."

As she pondered the possible limiting beliefs she might have, Kellie playfully reached over, picked up his top hat, and set it on top of her head. She glanced at Laurie and leaned back, putting one foot up on the carriage rail in front of her, interlocking her fingers together in her lap. "Hmm," she said. "Sounds as though we have some mental work to do. Anything else that might slow or stop us?"

He gazed out at the tree-dotted landscape for a moment, thinking. Then he continued. *"Timing plays a role, as well.*

For instance, both of your souls chose to be late bloomers. That was your plan from the beginning, it was one of the cards you each started your game with. You wanted that experience. Remember, the cards your soul chose will always overrule what your human self wants, and sometimes those cards affect when *things may happen. So with some cards, there may be a bigger delay than your human self would like. You might play The Creating Game today and not get what you want until next week, next year, or in ten years.*"

As they circled around a bend in the roadway, they saw a shining white curtain directly in front of them. Seraphina stopped.

He turned to face them. "*You don't need to understand or remember every exception to every rule. I'm telling you that right now, because for all of your questions, there will always be a rule and a number of exceptions. That's because life isn't that simple. I know you would like it to be, but it's just not. But as long as you remember the basic rule in question and play the game as best as you can accordingly, you'll be in better shape than most.*"

He lifted his hat from Kellie's head and placed it back on his own. Then he stood and stepped down to the ground, coming around to their side of the carriage and holding out his hand to help them down. "*I'm going to drop you off here because you're not ready to go where I'm headed just yet. But I want to remind you of the highlights from today so that what's important sticks with you.*"

After they had said their goodbyes to Seraphina, he hopped up into the carriage again from their side and turned to face them. "*If you want the Creating Game to work for you, you have to meet the Universe halfway. I'll help, but you have to meet me halfway as well. A lot of it is a mental game. Start by knowing you deserve it. I want you to have hope, goals, and things to strive for. It's part of your game to know that it is possible to achieve heath, make the money you want, and end up in a beautiful relationship.*

"So if the creating game gives you that hope, use it. If you just don't believe in it, then don't." He shrugged. *"But know this: If you are striving to reach a goal, if you want something you don't have at the moment, reach for it in a happy, positive state of mind. Then do the work to get it. I promise you, you'll be much more likely to obtain that goal, and to achieve it more easily, whether you believe in the Creating Game or not."*

He sat down, and the carriage began to move forward. They stood on the roadway, and heard the old man whistling "Stairway to Heaven" as they watched him disappear with Seraphina through the shimmering white curtain, leaving tiny glistening sparkles in the air as the curtain slowly disintegrated in the afternoon sunlight.

CHAPTER 16

Lake Tahoe, California

It was Saturday night and the brightly lit casino pulsed with excitement. The musical sound of slots and the low hum of voices were punctuated by the occasional excited yell or bell ringing when someone hit a jackpot. Kellie and Laurie were seated at one of about twenty blackjack tables, all of them full of players, the green felt on each table spread with colorful cards and stacks of chips.

Since both women worked from home, neither one of them dressed up often. Tonight they had taken advantage of the opportunity and were dressed in style: Laurie in a flowing green dress with sparkling black three-inch heels, and Kellie in a form-fitting black dress and matching heels. Both women sported dangling earrings and designer purses.

Laurie was on a roll. With plenty of psychic guidance, she was building up the winnings in record time. Kellie was enjoying her favorite drink, a Cadillac margarita, and watching the show. She took a long, slow sip, savoring the sweet and salty taste. It had been several weeks since she had visited Laurie in Manhattan, and now it was Laurie's turn to visit her in California. They had driven up from

Santa Cruz to Lake Tahoe earlier in the day, ready to spend a couple of days seeing the sights and having some fun. They were also hoping that the old man would invite them to call him in for a chat or two.

Several people were leaving the table and they gathered their chips, tucking them into pockets and purses. "Oh," Laurie said suddenly, "I meant to tell you: When you were in the shower before we left, I got a call from my client who put off doing in vitro for a month because the angels told her to, remember her?"

"I do," Kellie said. We've had our fingers crossed for two months. Did it work?"

"Yes! She's pregnant!"

"Whoo-hoo!" Kellie said enthusiastically. Two players at the table looked at her in mild annoyance. Uncaring, she held up her hand for a high-five and Laurie gave it a resounding smack.

Several people filled the recently vacated seats. The dealer distributed chips as requested, then began to shuffle the deck.

"How about your client who was dealing with the 'old boys club?'" Laurie asked. "How's she doing?"

"She's fabulous," Kellie said. "She stood up to them, exactly the way we practiced, and they backed off. They may still not be happy about having a woman in their ranks, but they respect her now and there appears to be a truce. She doesn't cry on the way to work anymore, and she feels good about herself and how she handled the situation."

"Yay!" Laurie said, approving. They high-fived each other again.

After shuffling, the dealer reloaded the shoe. Kellie

nodded at the table, and they both stopped talking and watched the play begin.

After another round of winning, Laurie got that *look*. Kellie recognized it instantly: Laurie had heard something with her talent that she didn't like and she wasn't happy. She stopped betting. Kellie put her drink down and said casually, "What's up?"

"My spirit guides say that's enough. They aren't going to help me win any more."

"Why not?"

Laurie paused, listening. Kellie waited patiently. How Laurie worked with the angels and guides was very familiar to her. Laurie went on: "They say I'm not supposed to use them to make big bucks. A little is fun, a lot isn't right. I'm not meant to win a lot of cash."

"Ask them if they'll let me do it then. They can help *me* win!"

There was another pause. Then, "They say nope, they're done for the evening."

Kellie pretended to look affronted. "Well! Alrighty then. So much for the novelty of bringing a psychic to Tahoe. Apparently divine guidance is no guarantee of riches."

Laurie grimaced. "Unfortunately not." She gathered up her chips, and they clacked together softly as she dropped them into the outside pocket of her purse. They stood up.

Kellie slung her purse over her shoulder and then remembered her drink as they were leaving. She went back to snatch it up. Wobbling slightly on the new high heels she was definitely not used to, drink in hand, she trailed behind Laurie. They were heading in the general direction of the front doors when suddenly, Laurie stopped and turned around, looking excited. "They said it's time for another meeting with God. They're telling me to call him in!"

Kellie looked pointedly around the casino, at her drink, then at her shoes, and said, *"Here?"*

"Yes. Believe it or not, here. They say they'll guide me to the right place after I call him in."

Kellie spotted a bench nearby and pointed. "Let's sit down. You can do it while I finish my drink." She wobbled over to the plush red bench and sat down, landing just hard enough for her drink to slosh a bit over the rim of the glass.

Laurie looked at her archly. "Perhaps you should dump the rest of the drink in the trash instead. After all, we *are* going to be speaking with God. Wouldn't you prefer to be on top of your game?"

Kellie glared at her, then sighed. With a wistful look at the green tinted liquid, she tossed it into the silver trash can next to the bench.

Laurie sat down beside her, closed her eyes, and began taking slow, deep breaths. "Okay. I'm going to need a whole lot of white light here, with some very bright silver and gold sparkles. There are a lot of people in this casino and I want to surround them all, starting with us. I'm covering everyone in beautiful white light, from the tops of their fancy hairdos to the bottoms of their expensive designer shoes. I'm filling this whole building up."

Kellie lowered her eyes and looked from beneath her lashes around the casino, to see if anyone was staring at them. It would be a little embarrassing to try to explain exactly what Laurie was doing. She supposed she could blame it on a little too much tequila, if she had to.

Laurie said in a whisper, "Yo, God, come in and give me a signal, please." In a moment, her eyes flew open. "Got it! Okay, follow me." She jumped up and began moving quickly toward the back of the casino. Kellie looked doubtfully at her friend's brisk pace, then looked down and eyed her new heels. Making her decision, she kicked off her shoes. She bent down to grab the shoes and her purse, then jumped up and took off after Laurie in her nylon-clad feet.

She caught up just as they passed through an archway in the casino. Immediately, all the lights dimmed. The musical sound of slot machines spinning and coins clinking became muted as though they were underwater. Momentarily confused, the two women stopped, looking around…

…And there he was, dressed to the "nines," wearing a black and white tux with black shoes that were so shiny, Kellie was sure she could freshen her make-up using them as a mirror.

He was sitting at a dollar slot machine, and as they watched, he casually popped in a coin and pulled down the handle. The pictures spun with the music and a black bar and two cherries rolled to a stop and lined up. He turned away from the machine, considering them. *"Having fun?"*

"We were for a while," Laurie said, scowling. "But apparently I'm not *allowed* to win big."

Ignoring her disgruntled comment, he said, *"Money is an interesting phenomenon. You humans never seem to manage it well. Even when you get to be a grownup, many of you act like the proverbial kid in a candy shop. You get cash and you spend it—or blow it, as the case may be—and then you say, 'Where'd it all go?'"*

"I don't think that's true for a lot of us," Laurie said

heatedly. "I think it's more like we never got enough to start with, and *then* it's 'Where'd it all go?'"

The women each selected one of the red vinyl-covered stools in front of the slot machines, sat down, and swiveled to face him. They set their purses on the floor between them, and Kellie dropped her shoes and kicked them next to the purses.

"*Most of you put yourselves in that mindset of, 'I never have enough, I never have enough,' and so that is what you create.*"

"You know what? I don't think that's true," Laurie said firmly. "It's not even about making a fortune. So many people have jobs where they simply get paid X amount an hour or X amount a month or whatever. How can we turn that into more? A lot of people don't even *have* jobs! And it seems as though the price of everything is just skyrocketing, especially housing."

Kellie got up and began following the large swirls in the blue patterned carpet, feeling the tough fabric through her nylons. "I have a client whose big dream is to buy a house, but housing prices, at least where I live in the San Francisco Bay Area, are just beyond reach for most. I don't see how people afford it."

"It's the same where I live, in Manhattan," Laurie said. "A dinky little condo is a million dollars. Who would have ever dreamt that?"

Kellie stopped, bent down, and picked up a coin that had fallen on the floor. She walked over and popped it into the nearest machine and pulled the handle. Shortly, a few silver coins clattered loudly down into the tray. She ran her hand through the coins without picking one up, and then turned around to face the old man. "Being a personal coach, money and cash flow is one of the primary issues that come up repeatedly for my clients. I'd love to have something positive to tell them, when they feel as though they are just struggling to survive. I need something helpful to say when they are trying to make enough to pay the electric bill and feed and clothe their kids, much less pay me. Most of them would really love to keep working with me for longer than they do, but the financial piece often limits them."

She threw her hands up in the air in a gesture of frustration. "And of course, as a coach, I encourage people to follow their bliss or to get a job doing what they love. But it's awfully hard to follow your bliss when you're just trying to scrape up enough to pay the rent."

Laurie reached over and picked up one of the coins in Kellie's tray. Flipping it into the air, she said, "No one I know feels like they make enough." The coin flashed in the air, spinning until she caught it.

CHAPTER 17

"**N**o one," Laurie finished flatly, holding the coin between her fingers and shaking it at him. "So how *do* you make enough, God? How do you do everything that you want to do in life? How do you lead a satisfying life and survive, especially with the cost of living going up and up and up and people having less and less because their income isn't keeping up?"

He shrugged. "*Right now, times are tough. Cash flow is tight for most. That is a big overall game, and it's not going to change any time soon.*"

He broke off as Laurie rolled her eyes at the ceiling.

Then, apparently deciding to ignore her, he continued: "*A lot of you are going to be forced to take a look at what's important to you and what's not important to you. At what you need; what you really, really want; and what you're wasting your hard-earned cash on. Many of you are wasting it. I'm not going to say if you buy X, that's a waste. The list is different for different people. But everyone is going to have to start thinking: 'What do I really need? What do I really want?' You'll have to pick and choose.*"

A coin appeared in between his fingers, and he flexed

them, the coin weaving in and out. He put it into the slot machine beside him and pulled the handle. *"Many of you are going to be forced to simplify your lives. You're going to have to cut back. The entire world will be changing. You're going to go back to a simpler time."* As he spoke, the five slots in the machine rolled to a stop, one at a time. The bar and cherries were gone.

Instead, two slots showed modest but attractive homes, two showed simple, wholesome meals on sturdy tables, and one showed a family relaxing under an umbrella at the beach.

Laurie frowned at the pictures. "So, you're telling us that we're just going to get poor and stay poor and be simple and not be able to go on nice vacations or whatever, and that nobody will be able to in the future?"

He raised his hands in a placating gesture. *"No, I'm not saying that at all. But I am telling you that you're going to have to start to think about what you need. And you know what? You might even need to go on some of those vacations. But the daily purchases that are not needed, the daily shopping trips that waste, waste, waste—those are going to have to go."*

Kellie brightened. "So it's only the overindulgence and the wastefulness that will have to go. Sounds as though it will help us focus on what's really important, so we learn to be happy without excess."

He nodded. *"Although money can certainly be a fun part of your game, living a fulfilled life and being happy is not necessarily about how much you have. But as long as you think it is, you'll be chasing money instead of changing your thoughts and attitudes so you're happy right now. And remember, like attracts like. One of the best ways to create more is to stop thinking, 'I never have enough,' and focus instead on what you have at the moment and be happy with it."*

Laurie thumped the closest slot machine with her fist. "I just so disagree, at least the part about the wasteful shopping trips," she persisted. "Because I'm thinking about my friends who are in my financial bracket. I don't see any of us going on huge shopping sprees or even buying expensive entertainment or liquor or whatever. I feel like you're talking to rich people when you talk about wasting money, not to us or most of our friends, or even our clients. I don't think 'cutting back' is going to solve the challenge."

Kellie sat down again on her stool, putting one foot up and curling her toes around the supporting bar underneath. "A lot of people complain about how they don't have enough, Laurie, but in my experience, it isn't always the ones who actually don't have enough. I know people who are very prosperous who talk and feel as though they don't have enough, and I know people who get by on very little and think they have plenty. So people's perceptions, or mindsets as he said," she nodded at the old man, "obviously have *something* to do with it."

"Still, I think the economy plays a big part." Laurie tossed her coin into the air again. "Yes, we know that it's all part of the game." She caught the coin, holding it out and pointing it at the old man. "And now you're telling us it's not going to change much. So what we're looking for is more guidance on how to play this 'Creating Money' game, because I think people might feel like, 'Gee, it's the game and we have to do something, but we can't do it. There are all these obstacles in our way.'"

His head was cocked as he listened patiently. "*If it was easy from the beginning, there'd be no game, now would there? Sometimes you have to work and build up to having what you want. Your job is to figure it out: 'How am I going to make enough to live in the big house on Main Street as opposed to the cottage on Elm Street?' And while you're figuring it out, you have to learn to live within your means until you create your dream. You have to live in that one-room apartment. Or, sometimes the jobs don't work out and you're not prosperous because you're not in the field you're meant to be in. So you need to figure* that *out and then do what it takes to get to where you're meant to be."*

He waved his right hand to emphasize his point. *"I realize you can't always just jump out of a field that's paying you—unless it's not paying you enough—to move on to what you're meant to be doing. I know this is a very difficult part of the game.*

"Money and lack of it is a big, big challenge. And by the way, debt is another big bucket of trouble. There are those who get caught in that trap and have to learn to pull themselves out."

"Well, God, why don't you fix it?" Laurie demanded. "You talk about tweaking things, why don't you fix it so it's easier? You could help us out more."

Unperturbed, he said, *"You'll always have enough for what you need."*

Laurie glowered at him. "You're not answering the question."

He sighed. *"Well, I'm not going to drop a sack of cash at anybody's door, unless you got the sack-of-cash soul card this time around, which the vast majority of people haven't. Even though occasionally you get to choose the easy money card, the rest of the time you have to figure out how to get the cash for yourself."*

She threw her hands up in the air. "Well, see, that's the thing. 'Figuring out how to get it' leads to half the problems in the world. How do you get it? Some people decide crime is the way to get it."

Kellie jumped up, went over and sat on the stool next to the old man. She swiveled so she was facing him, hands braced on either side of the stool. She leaned forward and said earnestly, "Or, let's say you do look at how you're going to get it. Yeah, you can focus on just, 'Okay, how am I going to bring in the most income?' And some people do. But what about everything else? Some people go for the higher income and are miserable, because they don't enjoy what they do. But what they really want to do doesn't pay enough for them to feed their family."

She leaned back and relaxed a bit. "Laurie and I are choosing our bliss. We're doing what we love. We are not doing something that makes us miserable just to earn more. Frankly, it seems to me, when I look at all the people I coach, the ones going for their bliss struggle the most with making a living. And the ones that make the most often aren't happy with their jobs, but they don't feel as though they can leave because they need the higher income. What is wrong with this picture?"

"Most souls usually choose at least one card that has something to do with money. Remember, each and every one of you is different. As it is with most issues, there are many different cards that might have been chosen. For some, the card is 'I'm in a job I don't care for. I get to figure out how to get happy and keep myself happy with where I am.'"

Another coin appeared in his hand, and he put it into the machine and pulled the lever. This time, pictures of grumpy looking people doing various kinds of work whirred to a stop. "*For others, the card is, 'I'm in a job I don't care for. How can I get out of this job, go pursue my dream job, and be able to pay the bills as well?' Sometimes, part of the plan that goes with the card is to suffer, go without, and never have enough, so that you'll appreciate it when you finally do.*"

He nodded toward a plump woman in black pants seated at one of the slots near them. She had a tray full of coins in front of her, and yet she looked as grumpy as the people in the pictures on the old man's' machine. "*Some of you will never have the amount you want. Some of you will have the amount you thought you wanted, and it's still just never going to be enough.*"

He shrugged. "*That's how your soul is developing. The money game is very, very difficult. It's one of the toughest parts of the game, because you can't always simply say, 'Okay, let me change my thoughts and I'll be happy.' Some of you might change your thoughts completely and still go to your job Monday through Friday, still get that same paycheck, except for once a year when you get a small cost-of-living raise and a Christmas bonus. You're still going to get that same paycheck, no matter what you're thinking.*"

Laurie made no effort to hide her irritation. "Well, I think we've kind of figured that out. We were hoping for some sort of guidance on how to get around that so we can actually make more money."

CHAPTER 18

"And some guidance on how we're supposed to know which soul card we have—so we know what we're supposed to do," Kellie added. "How do we *know* if we're supposed to go find our dream job, or, if we're supposed to learn to be happy where we are?"

Once again, he put a coin in the slot machine. Kellie couldn't figure out where the coins were coming from, since so far, he hadn't won any. They just seemed to be appearing in his hand right before he popped them in. This time, the far-left slot came up with a man smiling while he was talking on the phone at his desk.

The old man beckoned Laurie to come over. She got up, walked over and stood next to him. He directed her gaze to the picture. Kellie turned around to face the spinning slots.

"Step one," he began. *"Regardless of which cards you might have, change your attitude. Look for things to appreciate about the job you have. Look for ways to make it better, or more interesting. It might be that the person who works at the desk next to yours has a great sense of humor. It might be you have a nice view out the window in the break room. Whether you're supposed to stay and*

learn to be happy or go find your bliss, finding things to appreciate where you are will help a lot."

Laurie looked as though she was going to say something sarcastic, thought better of it, and held her tongue. The second spinning wheel on the slot machine came to a stop. It showed a picture of a woman staring out the window at a blue sky with white clouds, a dreamy smile on her face.

He continued in an instructional tone. "*Step two: Pay attention to your dreams. What have you always wanted to do? What would you do if only? If there were no obstacles and you could do whatever you wanted, what would that be? Go to your favorite place to reflect—the beach, the forest, the top of the biggest skyscraper, wherever—and look into your heart.*

"*If you're supposed to leave and go find your bliss, that's where you'll find your answer. It might take a few minutes, a few months, maybe even a year or longer. But the answer will come to you. You'll just know. Don't stress and worry over it. Trust your intuition and gut instincts. Trust your guidance. Trust* me, *because that's how I work: I'll let you know what you're supposed to do if you just ask, then get quiet and listen.*"

The third, fourth, and fifth wheels slowed, and stopped with a jerk, one right after the other. The third showed a picture of a driveway full of toys, clothes, and furniture. A woman was handing cash to a man as she pointed to a dinosaur Lego set. The fourth was a picture of a woman showing a young boy how to play the piano, and the last was a picture of a woman playfully chasing four young children. He went on: "*Step three: let's say you're a nine-to-fiver, you're getting the same paycheck, and it's less than what you need. It's time for you to think, 'Okay, I need more cash. What am I going to do?*'"

He gestured toward the remaining pictures. *"These are some real examples of what people have done: some of you have garage sales, some of you teach piano lessons, and some of you babysit."* As he mentioned each item, he pointed at the corresponding picture.

"I had a client sell clothes on eBay once to make enough to hire me," Kellie said, musing.

He made a fist and hit the palm of his other hand with a smack. *"There you go! Compared to the way it was fifty years ago, there are a multitude of opportunities out there to make more all by yourself and without a boss. You don't even have to have a garage sale. You can sell your trash to make more! You just might have to be creative. Maybe you need to learn to build something, clean something, or pick up how to do something else."*

He turned away from the pictures on the slots and faced Laurie, who was still standing there, looking at the pictures. He rubbed his chin thoughtfully as though he were thinking hard. *"There are many choices. For instance, one mother might think, 'Hmmm, there's not enough food for my children, what am I going to do?' She might sell her kids' toys and make a few bucks, or she might opt to sell drugs and make a few thousand dollars."*

Kellie whirled around, looking shocked. "I can't believe you said that! If she opts to sell drugs, she'll end up in jail, and then what are her kids going to do?"

He nodded. *"Exactly. Some have opted to make that choice in a moment of despair. That's why you always need to think long and hard before you make any drastic, potentially life-altering decisions."*

"I would think so!" She got up and, navigating around Laurie, began pacing again, back and forth this time. "I know I keep harping on this, but what about fulfillment? You can do all kinds of extra stuff to boost your income, but where's the satisfaction?"

Laurie shot Kellie an exasperated look. "I'd experience a great deal of satisfaction if you would just refrain from pacing all over the place," she said dryly. "I swear, sometimes I get dizzy just watching you."

"Walking helps me think. I ..."

A loud cry sounded nearby. Startled, Kellie stopped short and they all turned toward the sound. A man who looked as though he'd had a few too many had stumbled into a waitress carrying a tray full of drinks. She was trying to keep the tray upright as he grabbed hold of it to get his balance. The drinks tipped and appeared beyond saving.

Kellie was sure they were about to end up all over the poor waitress's white blouse. Then suddenly, the man let go and backed off. The tray stabilized, and the drinks sat quietly right where they belonged. The waitress looked confused, then relieved, and, straightening her blouse with one hand, quickly headed away toward her original destination.

Kellie turned her head and squinted in exaggerated suspicion at the old man, silently accusing him of being responsible for the good deed.

He looked innocently back at her—too innocently. *"Regarding fulfillment, I know this isn't what you expect me to say, but sometimes, money* will *fulfill you. Working at a job when you're not making enough will send you on the adventure of money fulfillment, which is the perfect adventure for many of you. You see—"*

"—That certainly works for me," Laurie interrupted. "I'm already doing what I love: helping people." She sat down on her stool, turning to face the old man again. "I'm more than ready for the adventure of money fulfillment, thank you very much. Bring it on!"

He gave her the same look a third-grade teacher might give a student who spoke out of turn. Then he went on. *"You see, a lot of you become complacent and just sit in that dead-end job forever and ever, until* something *makes you get up and move. Change is not something most people care for, so not making enough is often the one thing that gets you motivated.*

"Sometimes you don't make enough and you hate your job, and then you get out there and start to look, and you discover that: 'Hmm, this job isn't so bad. I'm making more than I would be making at all these other jobs that are even worse. Maybe I'll just have to stop buying steak and start buying baloney for a while to save up.' And that's the answer for some of you."

Kellie had gone back to pacing. "You said earlier that everyone has some type of soul card or cards related to money, and you've also mentioned that at one time or another, everyone gets to choose the 'easy money' card, correct?" she asked.

"Yes, the 'here's your sack-of-cash on a silver platter' card," Laurie added. "That's the one I want!"

"Yes, that's correct. Everyone chooses the easy money card at one point or another, but not every lifetime. So the steps I'm giving you here today are the steps you take if you don't have that card this time around, which many people don't."

"Hold on," Kellie said. "It's possible that someone might get the easy money card, but also have challenges with that card, isn't it? Because I've heard that rich people sometimes don't know who their true friends are. They don't know if they're liked for themselves, or for their wealth."

"Yes, that's definitely a challenge people with that card might have."

She stopped and crossed her arms. "So it's not all sunshine and roses, even if you have what looks like a lucky card this time around."

His eyes met hers. *"Nope,"* he said candidly. *"But where's the fun in a game with no challenges?"* he added. *"That would be boring."*

"True," Kellie said. "And besides, however you get it, working hard, or handed to you on a silver platter, you'll still have those particular challenges."

CHAPTER 19

"Let's get back to the whole how to make *more* of the green stuff, so we get to *have* those challenges, shall we?" Laurie said impatiently. "Just to be clear, there's nothing *stopping* us from making a lot just because we didn't get an easy money card, right? It's just that we have to figure out how to do it on our own?"

He nodded. *"That's right. In fact, even if you have a 'poverty' card, that doesn't mean you can't change that. It only means at some point you'll experience not having enough money. Your soul wanted that experience. How long you experience it is up to you. You can still work to change it successfully. Really, the only difference between having an easy money card and not having one, is if you have the card, you don't have to do anything. In fact, you can do absolutely nothing, and you'll end up wealthy—if you weren't already born into it. But don't forget what Kellie just said, being wealthy comes with its own set of challenges."*

Laurie rolled her eyes. "Yeah, yeah, I know, but I'm more concerned with where the rest of us are at right now. Most of my clients are in the same boat as I am. What if someone is in a job or career that's not paying well enough, and he—or she—wants to make a whole *lot* more, not just a little extra in addition to their job to be able to pay the bills. They want to go on the adventure of money fulfillment, as you put it. How do they do that?"

He looked at Kellie. "*You're an entrepreneur, Kellie. You've been one your whole life. You've had what, three successful businesses?*"

"Four, if you include a booming babysitting business as a teenager," she said cheerfully.

"*How would you answer Laurie's question?*"

She thought for a moment. "Be enterprising."

"*Very well.*" He opened his fist to reveal another coin, which he put into the slot machine and pulled the handle. All five slots rolled up and stopped at once. There was printing that ran across all of them. "What is this, google on steroids?" Kellie said, joking. She read the printing out loud. "Enterprising: 1) Ready to undertake projects of importance or difficulty, or untried schemes; energetic in carrying out any undertaking. 2) Characterized by great imagination or initiative."

"*In other words,*" he began, "*Some of you sitting in your one-room rental apartments saying, 'I'm creating the castle in the mountains,' will get it, because you're willing to do what it takes to get out there and create it. So go for it.*

"*Then there are those of you sitting there on your couch watching TV who say, 'I'm creating the castle in the mountains—hand me another beer and some chips—I'm creating the castle in the mountains.' Well, you might get the can of beer that says 'You are the million dollar winner,' but more than likely you won't. It's probably not going to come to you unless you hold up your end of the deal. That's how the game works. Get it?*"

"I get it," Kellie said. "Everything I've ever done, including create my businesses, has come because I've worked hard at it. I've been self-motivated and taken the initiative, which I've noticed a lot of people don't do."

He stood up, stretched, and then leaned back against the machines, crossing his legs at the ankles. "*Sometimes it's not even that difficult. How many stories have you heard about someone doing the Monday to Friday job thing, or whatever days they work, and that person suddenly had an idea that made him a million dollars? Imagine this: Joe is sitting at home, and I'm going to make this example up, he's sitting at home eating his crackers.*"

He tapped the side of his head with his forefinger. "*All of a sudden he thinks: 'I wish there were some crackers that already came buttered. That would be perfect! Then I wouldn't have to put in the effort to get the butter and spread it on the cracker. Sounds easy; why don't I just package up some crackers and butter?'*

"*Then he goes and talks to his buddy at the store on the corner, and his buddy says, 'Hmm, that's a good idea. Let's try it.' They work it out and package it, and then the following year they're sitting in their castle in the mountains up to their ears in crackers and butter! It doesn't always have to be work, work, work, think, think, think, create, create, create. Sometimes it can just be poof!*

"*Ideas like that come to everyone at one point or another, but ninety-five percent of you think 'Yeah, that would be cool' and then go back to your TV shows. It's the five percent that call up their buddies and get the ball rolling that get the castle in the mountains.*"

"I hate to rain on this parade," said Laurie, "but you *know* I've had ideas and acted on them, and they haven't ever amounted to a hill of beans. So it's not always that easy, and it doesn't always work."

"*No, it doesn't. At least not the first time, or the first idea. Sometimes you have to be persistent. Keep trying different ideas, or keep trying the same idea different ways, before you're successful. That's the game. You can ask Kellie about that one, too, she's had plenty of experience in that department.*"

Kellie looked at him ruefully. "Actually, I was going to say that *most* of the time it's not that easy. In most of my businesses, I've had to fail a whole lot at first, trying different things, until I finally hit on what worked. Persistence is key."

CHAPTER 20

"But what if you can't be persistent," Laurie said stubbornly. "If you barely have enough to pay the rent, then you certainly don't have enough to go out and get the butter and the crackers produced."

"Well, no, most people with ideas don't have the funds to put it together. Most of them go down to their buddy that runs the grocery store they've been going to for ten years and they say, 'What do you think of this idea? What if we try it and see if it works in your grocery store?' Then he'll say, 'Well, I know the man that owns the butter company. He's been a friend of mine since elementary school. As for the crackers, let's go down to Matilda at the bakery, and see if she can bake us some crackers instead of rolls like she usually does for me.'

"That's where most of you stop. You have the idea, but you don't know what to do next. You're also worried that somebody's going to steal it, which is certainly a possibility."

"And happens quite regularly," Laurie said.

"Yes, it does. But it's going to work for some of you. You'll be in business with the grocery store owner, Matilda the bakery woman, and the guy who has the cows that make

the butter. Sure, you won't get all the profit, but you won't have to do all the work either, and you won't have to come up with five cents to back it. You'll still end up in your castle in the mountains.

"But you have to put in the effort. You have to pursue the idea, and sometimes it's hard. It's time-consuming, and you don't get paid while you're putting it together. There would be a lot more of you who would go from poverty-stricken to millionaire if you just had the curiosity and courage to move forward on your ideas. You must have passion, you must have faith, you must have desire, because it's a tough path and it's hard to stick to.

"And you know what? Some of these crackers and butter ideas are going to be big flops and you'll lose your entire investment. Your first idea is not always going to work. But some people's first idea is the big one, and then their next ten ideas don't work. Either way, you have to play or you won't know."

He turned around and deliberately put a big handful of coins into the machine and pulled the handle. Nothing happened. *"Once you try an idea and it's a flop, next time you'll think, 'Hmm, what about a whole grain cracker with peanut butter and jelly on it?' You'll try it again. You'll already know how to go about it, so this time, it might be a success. And it might not. But you're playing the game, and you're learning the rules."*

"I'm going on my fourth idea, by putting all this information you're giving us into a book," Laurie said wryly. "I've learned a lot of rules. So I figure it's my turn."

"I like this answer a lot," Kellie said enthusiastically. She started pacing again, walking back and forth across the carpet and using her hands to express herself. "It makes sense to me, because of my own experience. And I'll tell you something else, Laurie, it really is easier to be successful after you've failed a few times. Because there are no failures, just lessons. It's like taking classes in college, except you're taking classes in real life. You learn what you need to know, and whatever amount you spent isn't lost, it's just what the lesson or class cost you, that's all." She grinned. "Some of the classes are more expensive than others, I'll grant you that. But sometimes you get a great lesson for almost nothing."

He smiled. *"That's a great way to look at it."*

"And one more thing," Kellie continued. "Just because you get the easy money card, doesn't mean you'll keep it all, right? I'll bet it works both ways. In fact, I've heard that a lot of people who win the lottery lose it all, because they don't know how to keep it. So that's another one of *their* challenges: figuring out how to keep it. But if it wasn't handed to you and you've figured out how to earn it for yourself, then you'll be a lot more likely to know how to keep it. Am I right?"

He winked at her. *"You're catching on."*

"I think I am too," Laurie said reluctantly. "The hand of cards your soul chooses before coming in has to be played, because your soul wants to make sure you have the experiences that will fulfill it. You must have the opportunity to make choices about how you'll respond to those experiences. Everyone gets some positive cards and some negative cards—at least we see them as being negative because we're human. We see them *all* as positive when we choose them as a soul, because the end result is they build character, depth, and wisdom." She paused, thinking, and then laughed. "So you could say, we're all playing blackjack with God, and those qualities are our winnings."

"*But*," Kellie said eagerly, "those cards don't necessarily dictate how your entire life will go! Not only do you get to choose how you will respond to each card, which is significant, but there's still a whole lot of your life that's a blank canvas, so to speak. You get to paint whatever you want on it, by being enterprising, and by choosing your perspectives, attitudes, and thoughts so they are positive, happy, and attract more happiness and fulfillment."

He began to walk away. "*I think my work here is done, for today.*"

"Wait!" Kellie said.

He paused to look at her, lifting an eyebrow.

"We've talked a lot about how to create money, so I just want to recap."

He waited patiently. "So," she said, "what you've said is that, for the moment, we need to learn to cut back and live within our means. We need to learn what's important and make the tough decisions. We might have to live where we don't really want to and work in a job we don't love, but if we're motivated we can change that."

She began pacing again. "We need to start looking for the silver lining and focusing on that, to help ourselves feel better right away and to get the creating game going, so positive things start flowing to us. If we need cash now, we need to figure out how to get it, like sell clothes on eBay or have a garage sale or whatever."

She stopped, thinking. Then she began moving again. "If we're not sure we are in the right job, we need to look inside of ourselves for the answer, reflect, and listen to what our heart is telling us. The answer will be there, even if it takes a little time. If it's time to search for a different job or career, then take steps to move forward on that goal."

"And if we're just sick and tired of not having money," Laurie said, stepping in, "and we want to go on the adventure of money fulfillment, we need to be creative and act on our ideas." She winked at Kellie. "Be enterprising."

Kellie grinned back at her. "And if we try something and it doesn't work, don't get discouraged and give up, keep trying. Keep trying to do it different ways, try different things, or both. Persistence is key. Any money or time spent is just what we paid for what we learned. We're in the school of life. And sooner or later, we *will* succeed!"

They both turned to look at the old man. He gave them a thumbs up. "*Very good, start to finish. Did you note that I've been putting coins in during this entire discussion, and haven't won a single pot?*"

They both nodded.

"I don't want you to think I'm advocating gambling as part of your strategy," he said, "*but tonight, it works as a metaphor.*" He walked over and put one more coin into the closest slot machine and pulled the handle. "*Persistence is key.*"

Then he winked at them and walked away, melting into the crowd as the jackpot bell rang out. An avalanche of shiny silver coins cascaded down, filling the metal tray and then overflowing, raining down onto the carpeted floor.

PART IV

THE KARMA GAME

CHAPTER 21

Santa Cruz, California

"But it's not *fair!*" Aron's flair for drama was evident. If only he would dial down the volume. Kellie put her fingers in her ears. "I did all my chores," he protested. "Why do I have to do Kyle's too?"

"Your brother is sick. When you weren't feeling well, he did your chores. It all evens out in the long run. Sometimes I ask you to do more, sometimes I ask him to do more."

"How do I know it evens out? I don't know that," he stormed. Kellie sighed. "Just do it, Aron, okay?"

"Can I have extra screen time if I do?"

"Half an hour more, that's it. It's a school night."

"Oh, all right," he said, not very graciously. "I'll do the extra chores. Then can I play video games?"

"Yes," she said, heading for the stairs. She and Laurie had been back from Tahoe for a couple of days, and were ready for more information. Laurie was upstairs in Kellie's office preparing psychically for their next encounter with the old man. Assuming she had been able to concentrate, Kellie thought dryly. She hoped Laurie had added an extra measure of white light around the boys.

As she opened her office door, her forward momentum carried her not into her office but through the familiar shining white door. She stumbled in surprise as she found herself inside a large building with high ceilings.

The first impression that hit her as she stopped, disoriented, was of a very large space filled with a lot of beautiful carved wood. As her eyes adjusted to the dim light, the wood shapes became clear. There was a beautiful balustrade running the length of the room in front of her. It was basically a fancy, three-foot-high fence with ornately carved pillars and a smooth railing on top. The dark wood was polished to a glimmering sheen. She shivered, rubbing her forearms for warmth. The building felt colder than her house had been.

Beyond the balustrade, she saw several benches, a table and five chairs, and what looked like a three-sided cage about four feet high, open at the top. Past those items, she saw an imposing, carved wood wall with a long judges' bench and three chairs.

Laurie was sitting in the middle chair. The walls all around the inside of the building were either carved in the same wood or painted to match. On the far-right side of this odd setting was a set of three-tiered wooden jury benches, with a solid back and sides, so the tiered benches were essentially all one piece.

The old man was sitting on the bottom jury bench. He was wearing the black robes of a judge and a wig of curly white hair that went just past his shoulders. Noticing Kellie's shiver, he waved his hand. A faint humming sound began, and the walls, furniture, virtually everything solid in the room took on a faint red glow. As the humming grew louder and the red glow increased, Kellie felt warmth permeate the air. She stopped shivering.

She nodded at the old man. "Thank you."

He nodded back. The humming faded and so did the red glow, but the warmth remained.

Laurie looked down at Kellie gravely from her high seat. Then she pretended to pick up a judge's gavel, and, looking at Kellie with a mock stern expression, she struck the imaginary gavel on the table in front of her. It made a loud sound, just as though a real gavel had actually struck the table. She started, looking over at the old man. He winked at her.

She turned back to Kellie. "You have been accused of the crime of high treason against the United States of America. What do you have to say for yourself, miscreant?"

After a barely perceptible pause, Kellie fell to her knees, wringing her hands in front of her. "Oh sir, please, sir, it was an honest mistake, truly!"

"How so?" Laurie demanded.

Still wringing her hands in mock distress, Kellie said, "I was so intent on getting to the charity event on time, you know, the one to help the widows and orphans, that I plum forgot to put the money into the meter. But I had no intention of committing treason, not at all, no sir, not me!"

Laurie's lips quivered for just a moment, then her stern expression was back. "Nevertheless, treason it was, and therefore you must be punished!"

"Nooooo," Kellie wailed convincingly. "Please, I have a family! I have children—" she broke off suddenly, tilting her head, considering. "Come to think of it, I have not one, but *two* tweens, on the brink of becoming teenagers! What's the punishment for high treason? A quiet cell where no one will ask me for money, blast the TV at high volume, or drink the last of the milk and then put the empty carton back in the fridge?"

Laurie choked, her stern expression wavering again.

"Your honor, I'm guilty as charged." Kellie declared. She held out her hands in front of her, ready to be manacled in chains. "Please, take me away."

Recovering quickly, Laurie glared at her, picked up her pretend gavel and banged it again. Once again, it made a realistic sound. Without pausing a beat this time, Laurie announced, "No cozy cell for you, scoundrel. I sentence you to death for the crime of high treason!"

"What?" Kellie jumped up. "This is an outrage! I demand justice. I demand a punishment that fits the crime. Lock me away in a nice, quiet cell and throw away the key!"

Laurie stood up as well, shaking her imaginary gavel at Kellie. "You want justice? A punishment that fits the crime? Very well! I sentence you to life with two teenagers, with no chance of parole!"

Kellie froze in mock horror. Then, with extravagant melodrama, she wailed and moaned, collapsing to the floor in a heap of woeful misery.

"*Just don't forget to pay the parking ticket before your sentence is carried out,*" the old man said dryly. And both women finally dissolved into a fit of laughter.

When they had recovered, Kellie stood up again. The old man looked at her and waved his hand to indicate the room. "*Do you recognize this place?*"

"Actually, I do. It's the original courtroom inside Independence Hall in Philadelphia. We visited Philadelphia when my boys were toddlers, and I remember it."

"*I thought you might. That was a fun trip for you, wasn't it?*"

"It was! So, what are we doing here?"

"*Remember when I explained how the Creating Game*

was like a computer program running in the background of the soul's game?"

"Yes."

"Well that's not the only program running in the background. There's another one, and it's called, 'What you do comes back to you.' That's what we're doing here," he said cryptically.

When he didn't elaborate, Laurie eyed the caged structure and shuddered. "That thing gives me the heebie-jeebies."

"The founders were very proud of this place. It meant a lot to them, and rightfully so," he said thoughtfully. *"By the way, that's called a prisoner's dock, Laurie. That's where the accused would stand during the trial. It's actually where the term 'standing trial' came from."*

Kellie grimaced. "Now *I* have the heebie–jeebies."

"It was a lot better than what they'd been used to, trust me."

"Oh, I don't doubt it," Kellie assured him. "So, we're here to learn about 'What you do comes back to you.' Sounds like the concept of karma to me. That's something many Eastern religions talk about a lot. They say that whatever you do, good or bad, positive or negative, you get paid back in kind either in the same life or in another one. Are you telling us that karma actually exists?"

As she spoke, Kellie walked around the gleaming balustrade and pulled out one of the chairs from the table, straddling it as she sat down.

"It exists," he said, *"but karma doesn't come back as directly as some people think. It's not that if you hit somebody in the eye in this lifetime you're going to get hit in the eye the next lifetime, or later on in this one. In other*

words, just because you poked out someone's eye doesn't mean you'll have yours poked out. But twenty years later you might have a child who ends up blind.

"I'd also like to point out that karma is usually spoken of as if it were a punishment, but that's not how it's meant to be. It's not like that. It's really just another lesson that your soul has chosen to experience. It's also a question of fairness and that's why we're here today: The process that began in this room and endures today in this country was founded on the principle of fairness.

CHAPTER 22

"So many people say, 'Life's not fair. Things aren't fair,' the old man continued. "Actually, things are much fairer than you think. You can tell Aron I said that, by the way. More often than not, the consequence of a deed will happen during the exact same lifetime, even though it may not be exactly the same as the deed. For instance, there's a woman who left her lover without any explanation or even saying goodbye. It was cruel. She just disappeared. Years later, her car broke down in the desert and she was stuck there for five days without water. The one was a consequence of the other."

"Whoa, hold on," Kellie said. "First of all, even if it is fair, what is the point? That woman can't possibly know the reason she was stuck in the desert for five days was because she left her lover without a word years earlier. Second, I'm already getting confused between karma, and what we decide as souls before we're born. If we choose certain soul cards, or experiences we want as a soul ahead of time, and then it's all about how we play them during our life, how does that fit in with this karma thing? Are we

133

having experiences because we chose them, or are they a karmic result of our deeds?"

The old man held up both of his hands in a placating gesture. *"Let's take these questions one step at a time, okay? Let's begin with my explaining exactly how the process works when a soul chooses his or her hand of cards. Then I'll be able to show you how karma and fairness fit in with that. Okay?"*

Kellie nodded. "Okay."

Still in a playful mood, Laurie rose from the high judge's seat and then jumped down each stair with both feet at once, until after six thumps, she reached the jury bench where the old man sat. She plopped down at the far end of the bench, put her left arm across the back, and waited expectantly.

He paused for a moment. *"I'm thinking about how to explain this."*

While they waited, Kellie jumped up and began pacing toward the balustrade and back to the table again.

He seemed to have come to a decision. *"All right. I'm going to give you an example, a representation of what it's like when your soul chooses the cards to play your game."* He waved his hand, and with a peal of angelic bells, five people appeared in the chairs around the table. They were slightly transparent, just barely enough to know they weren't actually there in the flesh. One of them was clearly a depiction of the old man. One was Laurie, Kellie realized with a start, and one was Archangel Michael in glowing white robes. There were two others present: a dark-haired man, and a short, petite blond. She didn't recognize either one of them.

"Please don't take this literally," he began. *"We don't actually sit in chairs around a table. I'm simply presenting*

how it works in a way that's easy for you to understand. I'm going to use Laurie in this example, or Laurie's soul before she was born. You both know me, of course, and Archangel Michael. The two others are personal guides of Laurie's for this lifetime."

The figures were deeply engaged in animated discussion. Laurie's soul appeared to be very confident and enthusiastic. The others seemed to be presenting ideas and perspectives for her to consider.

Looking satisfied with his handiwork, the old man said, *"When a soul is choosing cards for the game of life, we help you as a group to plan. Except on rare occasions, you make the ultimate decisions, while the rest of us give input, steer, and guide you. The group consists of myself and the soul, and one or two beings who will be your personal guides in the coming life. Sometimes there's an archangel, sometimes Jesus may pop in. Different souls have different groups of angels joining in the discussion and helping them."*

He pointed to soul-Laurie, who looked to be passionately arguing a point. *"The first thing I want to get across to you is how much confidence your soul has. As a soul, you are often very gung-ho about choosing your experiences. For instance, you might say, 'I'm so good at life, I can do it with one hand tied behind my back!' So you choose to lose an arm to try it that way. In other words, the things you think are so 'bad' as humans have often been chosen because your soul* wants *the challenge."*

Archangel Michael had drawn what looked like a diagram on a piece of paper and was showing it to soul-Laurie. Everyone at the table stopped speaking, remaining silent as she reflected. *"Now, there are some souls who might opt for just the more positive experiences in a particular life if we didn't have the discussion. But they usually understand the value of the tougher challenges and know how beneficial they are, so after the big discussion they end up choosing a handful of cards that include both the more positive items* and *the tough challenges, maximizing their coming experience on earth."*

Soul-Laurie was nodding her head now, looking eager. He went on, *"When we're done with the discussion, the soul's attitude is like that of a kid getting ready to do an obstacle course. She's excited, thinking: 'Let me see if I can do this.'"*

The two women had been so absorbed by the scene and by his explanation, they had momentarily forgotten to ask questions. Now, Kellie said, "I see. So they're not sure they can do it? They might have a hand of cards that they may not be able to play successfully?"

He shook his head. *"No, that's not true. Every one of your souls believes they can master the challenges, or they wouldn't have taken them on. You don't ever choose a card you don't think you can win with. Yes, you'll have to be a detective and figure it out once you get there. No, it's not going to be easy. That's the challenge part. But I can't emphasize this enough: There is always an answer. Always. If you're playing the game and you feel stuck, remember that."*

"Okay," Laurie said. "So now, how does karma fit in with all of that?"

"Remember, the name of the game is to ultimately experience every single thing, positive or negative. So karma is just another one of the factors in the big discussion. Part of choosing your hand of cards is to consider what kind of karma you have.

"If you'll recall, your soul usually wants to experience the other side of whatever you've done anyway. So when you don't *experience the other side during the same lifetime, more often than not, you'll pick a card to experience the other side within the next couple of lifetimes."*

"And now we're back to my original point," Kellie said. "How fair is that? Whether it happens in the same lifetime, or several lifetimes later, we still don't even know it's something that's come back to us. How can we learn anything from that?"

The old man waved his hand again, and with a barely perceptible chime of bells this time, the tableau of characters around the table faded away. *"No, you don't necessarily learn anything or 'get it' as a human, and I know it doesn't seem fair from the human perspective. But as a soul, you learn an enormous amount, especially when your original actions and the karmic consequences are a couple of lifetimes apart. The timing works better for the soul that way. You learn more. It gives you a whole different awareness and knowledge."*

"Lovely," Kellie said sardonically. She stopped pacing and stood facing him, hands on her hips. "So once again, our almighty souls are reaping the oh-so-wonderful 'benefit' and we humans are stuck holding the bag. I'm sorry, I know I'm being difficult about this, but I've *always* thought the whole idea of karma wasn't fair. Now I have the chance to say so. You say it's fair to the soul, but so what? It's not fair to us humans! You say that sometimes it comes back to us in the same life. That woman that experienced her car breaking down in the desert for five days because she left her lover, or the one who has a child that's blind because she poked someone's eye out—c'mon, they don't make the connection! They can't! And if they don't make the connection, they're not learning anything."

"*You know what?*" He shot back, unperturbed. "*They may not say it out loud, but a lot more of them realize it than will admit it. For a lot of them, they know it subconsciously, just below the surface, that this thing is happening to them because of something unkind they've done in the past. But they certainly aren't going to say to anyone, 'I know I got stuck in the desert because I broke up with Steve without telling him.'*"

The old man leaned back, resting his arm on the back of the bench. "*And you're right, Kellie: Some will never get it. But it doesn't matter—it's still fair. If someone does horrible things, it's fair to experience a bit of that in return. Let's say John did one mean thing after another with his business, firing people who didn't deserve it, cheating, and stealing from his customers. Then years down the road, his business just fails, or the whole place catches on fire and he doesn't have any insurance, something like that. Trust me, he gets it. He would never admit it, but he gets it. A lot more of them get it than you think.*"

Laurie leaned forward, putting an elbow on one knee and resting her chin on her fist, observing the interaction. She appeared to be enjoying this role-reversal immensely. Kellie was usually the logical, wise, level-headed one. But when she got fired up about something, there was no stopping her. And she was definitely fired up about this.

"Well, what if it's a consequence from something done in another life?" Kellie threw her arms in the air. "For sure they are never going to get it, because they don't even remember that past life when they first did the deed. And you're a totally different person in another life, aren't you?"

He nodded. "*Yes, you are totally different. I mean, obviously you have the same soul, but you are a different person. And your memories don't cross over.*"

She crossed her arms, clearly with an attitude. "So. It hardly seems fair to have something bad happen to us in this life because of something some other person with the same soul did in another life that we don't even remember!"

There was silence. Laurie first looked at the ceiling, then with exaggerated care picked some imaginary lint off her shirt.

The old man softened his voice and leaned forward toward Kellie as he replied, "*I know it doesn't seem fair, and it's very hard for you humans to see this, because you don't recall those lifetimes. But you as a soul do see it differently. It's your goal to do everything, try everything, and experience everything. You'll choose to be everything that you hate and everything that you love. You'll think, 'Hmm, let's be the one that shoots somebody.' And then, 'Hmm, let's be the one that gets shot.' Just like a little kid: 'You know, I want chocolate this time. Next time, I'll want vanilla.' It's just like that.*"

CHAPTER 23

K ellie sighed. "It always comes back to the game." She began pacing back and forth again. "So the bottom line is that a 'bad' thing that happens to you is never a punishment. It's either a guided choice to gain the benefit from a particular experience, or it's karma to balance things out so they're fair, or both, right?"

"Yes. And, there seems to be a lot of focus on the negative consequences of your actions here, so I want to point out that there are just as many positive consequences from kind, positive things a soul has done, in this life or in a past one. You're just as likely to have a life where everyone wants to help you because you were helpful to others several lifetimes ago. What goes around always comes around, and, that includes every single positive thing you do. So remember that as well."

Laurie sat up straight and said brightly, "So if in some past life we were generous with others, then it's possible that in another one, people might be generous with us?"

"Yes, that could happen."

"So it could balance out."

"It could."

Kellie looked at her wryly. "Maybe so, but I still think that it's rotten for the one getting the consequence of some really bad karma, when the former self in another life did the deed."

The old man nodded. "*Speaking to you as a human, yes, it is rotten. When I speak to you as a soul, however, it's a whole different ball game.*"

Kellie walked over to one of the chairs, sat down, leaned back, and crossed her legs. She regarded the old man with an unreadable expression. "You know, all of this is very hard for us to hear. I mean, we're who we are, and ever since we began speaking with you, you've been telling us that our souls want things, things that are so different; things that we don't like as humans. It's hard."

The old man was silent. He simply gazed at her with those intense, wise, compassionate, all-knowing brown eyes of his.

"Well," she said finally, "help us understand more about the soul then. Tell us more about what it's like when you speak to one of us as a soul."

His voice was rich with compassion. "*There's a broader knowing. There's a deeper understanding. It's something that a human would have an extremely tough time comprehending.*"

"Will we ever blend with that soul and have all the knowingness that our soul has?"

He shook his head "*Not in human form. Your human forms are becoming more and more advanced, it's true, but you'll never remember as a human what you remember in soul form.*"

"Well, what about after we die? Do we blend with our souls and know everything our soul knows?"

"At different points in your evolution as a soul, you do realize and understand all of the lessons, all of the experiences, and all the feelings and emotions that you've gone through in your human lives. But never when you're on the earth in human form."

Kellie bit her lower lip, concentrating. "Will we remember all of our past lives and incarnations when we're in soul form?"

"When you advance far enough to sit at my right hand—and there's only a very few who have made it to that point so far, just because there hasn't been enough time—you'll have all of the knowledge from all of those lifetimes. Even some of the higher angels, the archangels, have all of that knowledge. Understand, though, that it's not as though they sit around chatting, saying: 'Oh, yeah, back in the year of this, I was that, and back in the year of this, I was the other.' They don't recall the thousands of lifetimes in detail. But they do bring back all of the knowledge."

Laurie looked surprised. "They don't even have a favorite personality they can remember?"

"Well, yeah, of course they could. It's not as though they don't remember anything at all. They can recall quite a few personalities, events, and parts of lifetimes. They just don't remember them all in detail."

"Do they have a personality that's a blend of all those personalities that they've been?" Laurie asked.

"More often than not. Because even the people you humans think were the worst, most horrible criminals may have had some positive personality traits."

"I see," she said thoughtfully. "So, being the humans that we are, even someone that we would consider evil might have good parts of that personality blended into the whole complete soul, right along with their other personalities and lifetimes."

"*Yes.*"

There was a short silence, then Kellie said, "Okay, I have one last question about karma."

"*Fire away,*" he said, his fathomless brown eyes piercing and alert as always.

"What if someone does something we would consider negative, but their motivation was positive? For example, they stole bread to feed a starving child? Or they lie, not to cover themselves, but to protect their child, or someone's feelings, or to keep someone else's sacred trust?"

"*The motivation behind the act is very important. It's always taken greatly into consideration,*" he said.

"And is that true the other way around as well?" Kellie asked.

"*It is. If a human performs what looks like a positive act, but the motivation is greed or something equally self-serving, that is taken greatly into consideration as well. It works both ways. It wouldn't be right for it not to.*"

"So sometimes," Kellie said carefully, "white lies really are not such a bad thing, and sometimes, being nice to someone so they will do something for you isn't such a good thing."

"*That's true.*"

She paused for a moment. "You do know that some of the religious leaders on the planet say the opposite, right? They say it's the action that counts, whatever the motivation was. So if you have good intentions but your action is not considered to be a good thing, your intentions don't matter."

"*As I've said before, what your leaders say is not always straight from me. So as you're given the instructions about how to live, how to think, how to do whatever, remember that those instructions are coming from another human. Although they often have many wise things to say, you don't have to follow everything you hear exactly. The best practice is to check your own inner guidance and intuition about anything you hear or read. If it doesn't feel right, let it go. If it feels right for you, then embrace it."*

"And I know that's what you want us, and other people to do with the information we're receiving from you as well," Laurie added. "Right?"

He inclined his head toward her. *"That's exactly right, Laurie."*

"Speaking of which," Kellie said suddenly, "We *are* very grateful for all of the information you've shared with us. We really appreciate your willingness to spend so much time with us, talking to us, explaining things, and being so patient. Right, Laurie?"

Laurie hesitated, but only for a moment. "Yes, of course."

"You're very welcome," he said. *"Thank you both for your willingness to communicate all of the information to others for me. I really appreciate both of you. You got that?"*

"Got it!"

"Yeah, got it, thanks."

He smiled and faded away, then the whole room faded. They found themselves back in Kellie's office, the only evidence of their adventure a final soft chime of bells, and a shower of tiny silver sparkles falling like indoor rain.

PART V

THE DEATH GAME

CHAPTER 24

May, 2006
Santa Cruz, California

"He says we can choose the place to meet this time," Laurie said.

They were lying opposite each other in the large hammock in Kellie's backyard. Putting their talks on hold during the busy winter, Laurie had opted to come out to sunny California again to resume them. Relaxing in shorts, t-shirts, and bare feet, they sipped wine out of crystal glasses, trying not to move too much so the hammock didn't deposit them in a heap on the ground.

"He says we can choose the place to meet this time," Laurie said.

"Why?"

"Because he wants to get into some heavy topics, and he wants us to be as relaxed and as comfortable as possible."

"Do we get to choose the topics?"

"Yes, although he always seems to know what we're going to ask, doesn't he? If he wants to add anything, he will."

"Where do you think we should go?"

"Hmm. Well, we haven't been to the beach yet. I've been looking forward to that since I arrived here, and the sound of waves is very soothing."

"Yeah, but a lot of the beaches around here are crowded, even at this time of year. Do we really want a bunch of people around when we discuss heavy stuff? We could ask him to make the door appear and take us somewhere deserted in the South Seas."

"Yeah, we could. But since I'm visiting you here in this lovely beach town, I'd like to see a West Coast beach. Aren't there any beaches reasonably close that are nice and not crowded?"

"Actually, come to think of it, there's one I know of. We'd have to climb down a steep embankment, at least if we go the usual way. But it's lovely, off the beaten track, and not well known."

"Let's go the usual way. I want to see more of Santa Cruz."

Kellie took a sip of wine. "Works for me!"

Early the following morning, after dropping the boys off at a friends' house, they drove up the coast. It was a sunny day, and spring was in full bloom, with greenery and flowers galore. Pulling over onto a dirt road, they parked the car and walked over a set of train tracks, carrying the chairs slung across their backs. Standing at the top of the cliff, they gazed down at beautiful, deserted Panther Beach. The blue-green waves rolled in and crashed rhythmically, the morning sun shining in a long arc across the water. Then they slid, more than climbed, down the steep embankment. Fortunately, Kellie had warned Laurie to wear running shoes. They were careful to avoid the occasional shrub that stretched its scratchy tentacles into the pathway, making sure their t-shirts didn't snag and protecting their bare legs below cut-off jeans. They reached the bottom and began walking toward the ocean.

Laurie looked around, drinking in the view from the bottom. "It's beautiful! I love that stone archway over there. It frames the ocean perfectly, just as though you're looking through nature's window."

"I know, right? And look, there's no one here."

"Where shall we sit?"

"Let's go where we can see the ocean through the archway while we talk."

They set up three chairs facing the ocean, so they could look out at the waves during the session, and sat down, leaving the chair in the middle for the old man.

"Okay, now what?" Laurie asked. "Where is he?"

"Oh! Look." Kellie pointed to the ocean, and there was the old man emerging from the waves, shedding water and wearing blue swimming trunks with a large shark on them, mouth wide open, sharp teeth gleaming wetly in the sun.

"Nice trunks," Laurie commented when he approached.

"*Thank you,*" he said with some amusement. "*I like them.*"

Laurie frowned. "Wouldn't something more somber be appropriate for a 'loaded topic' day?"

"*Absolutely not. These are perfect.*"

"Okay, if you say so."

He walked over and sat down between them on the empty chair. "*I do say so.*" He looked at Laurie expectantly.

"What? Why are you looking at me?"

"You know why. You've had something on your mind for a long time now, and it's about time you finally brought it up. This is the perfect day. I know you've been thinking that as well. It's time to come clean."

She hesitated. Then she took a deep breath. "Okay, but you know you aren't going to like it."

"I want to hear it."

There was silence. The ocean breeze blew softly past them, gently ruffling their clothing. Kellie looked at Laurie curiously.

Laurie appeared to be having an internal struggle. Finally, she said, "Fine. This is something that's been on my mind for the last thirty years. I was having such a tough time in college and one day I said, 'God, if you really want to hurt me, why don't you just take someone from my family?' And the next night my grandfather died suddenly. He wasn't even sick! He died suddenly of a heart attack."

Unexpected shock vibrated through Kellie. Horrified and hardly daring to breathe, her eyes were riveted on her friend. So *that's* what she's been so angry about, she thought. *That's* what's been eating at her ever since we first made contact with God!

Raw pain etched the features on Laurie's face. "How could you? How could you do that to me? To him? I've never gotten over that. I've been listening to everything you've said, and I'm still so pissed off at you. Did I choose that? I can't imagine why.

"Maybe my soul chose it, who knows? What lesson would there be for my soul to learn by being pissed off at you? Did you do that because I challenged you?"

"No. I would never be hateful in any way. Laurie, that was simply your grandfather's time to go. It had been

planned for sixty years that he would die at that particular age, and the heart attack was simply a good opportunity to make his exit. He did not die because you said that to me. Let's get that straight."

"How could there be such a coincidence? That has messed up my relationship with you for so long. I don't understand how I could say that and then have it happen the next night, and that it could be just a coincidence. It was such a sudden, unexpected death. I just don't get it." She spat the last few words out, like a tea kettle coming to a boil and spitting out bits of steam before the whistle sounds.

"It's all part of your soul's game plan. You chose to have that experience. You've had an attitude toward me for most of your life. Do you think you would have challenged me as much as you have otherwise? And you still haven't let loose on me yet." He leaned forward intently, continuing to look at Laurie while he said, *"Kellie, you give me a lot more emotion than Laurie does. Laurie is very controlled."*

Laurie's face looked as though a summer storm was raging beneath the surface. "You're telling me to open my mouth and let loose, and yet I'm talking to the greatest thing—you. Even though I am seriously angry about quite a few things, I have this respect thing, and I don't know . . . I just don't know about . . ."

"I'm giving you permission to let loose. That's what your problem is: You never let loose. The anger just leaks out in cynical, snide comments. You never let it all out until it's too late and you just about pop. You and I are meant to butt heads, Laurie. And, part of your soul's plan is to learn to muster up enough courage to stand up for yourself. So often you pull this," his tone of voice suddenly changed to a high-pitched, little-girl voice, *"'I don't know, I don't*

know' thing. I've heard many humans say that when they get uncomfortable. Whenever they get nervous, they opt for the little child 'I don't know.'

"Put your big-girl panties on, Laurie. You are the strongest, most powerful warrior. You don't think I've heard the conversations you've had with others about me? You think you can actually talk behind my back? Why don't you have those conversations directly with me?"

Kellie was still frozen. He appeared to be deliberately provoking Laurie. Probably to get her to let it all out, she thought. Not moving a muscle, her eyes stayed locked on Laurie's to see how she would respond.

CHAPTER 25

"Fine," Laurie fired back at him, standing up and giving the beach chair a savage kick in his direction. "I've got an attitude toward you. I think you spend your time up there scratching your dick, looking down and saying, 'Ho, ho, ho. Watch this.' That's what I've thought over and over and over my whole damn life. It's like you're up there saying, 'Watch the tsunami. This is going to be the really big game.' That's what I picture you up there doing every day: scratching your dick, looking down, saying, 'Ha. Watch this shit.'"

"Oh, man, now we're going to have to X-rate this book," Kellie said under her breath.

But Laurie heard her. "Well, he's inviting me to say what I really and truly think!"

"Oh, no question," Kellie said hastily. "He definitely wants you to let loose. I'm cringing over here, but I agree, you should go for it. Get it out!"

"It's not just Louisiana and the hurricane," Laurie continued. "You do it over and over and over. Okay, yes, maybe all those people opted to lose every damn thing, just like all the people in the tsunamis, but *damn*, do you have to make us suffer this much? I'd like to hear how some of the hurricane victims would explain how they felt. I'd love to talk to some of the people that were stuck in the water in New Orleans, just to hear the wording they would choose to describe the experience."

The old man was as calm as ever. He could have been relaxing at a Sunday picnic. "*I know you're angry with me. You're not the only one. There are many, many people who are angry with me. Why do you think you're the one I've chosen to receive my message?*"

He waved his hand in a large, sweeping arc all the way around. "*You speak for all of them. Do you think you would be in this position today, having had all of these heated debates and preparing to spread my word, if you hadn't been so angry with me? As I said, we were meant to butt heads. Otherwise, there would be no book.*"

Kellie swore she could see steam coming out of Laurie's ears.

"Thirty years of *hell* so I could write a *book* for you?" Laurie said incredulously.

"*No,*" he said. "*Thirty years to prepare you for your destiny, Laurie. You were meant to do this work for the world.*"

Laurie was speechless with shock. She simply stared at him.

"*And now, you're receiving the answers,*" he said gently. "*I've said it before, and I'll say it again: It's all a piece of the picture to help you grow. It's all a piece to give you depth of character. It's all a piece to fulfill the soul. It's all a piece of fulfilling that curiosity the soul has to know every single feeling, every single emotion. That's all it is. Plain and simple. I get that you don't like it. But that's how it is.*"

Still speechless, Laurie turned around, gave the sand

a kick even more ferocious than the one the chair had received, and stormed off. Kellie moved to follow her, but the old man said, *"Leave her alone. Let her walk it off. She'll be back."*

♦ ♦ ♦ ♦

"I'm concerned," Kellie said.

"She'll be fine," the old man replied.

"Not about Laurie, about something else."

He looked at her, quirking an eyebrow questioningly.

"I agree that people need to get things out, communicate their feelings, and not hold it in. And I'm glad Laurie finally spoke up. However, not everyone can stay as objective as you can in the face of another person's anger. And there are some people . . . well, if you tell them to communicate their feelings and they do, it's more of a dump than a communication. In other words, they'll say, 'You made me angry. It's all your fault.

"'You shouldn't have' —and then out comes whatever it is they are blaming on the other person. And of course, that doesn't make things better, it usually makes things worse."

"I hear you," he said. *"It's true."*

"So," she said, "I think when we tell people about this, and I'm sure we will, we should at least mention that it's not just about saying how you feel to people, it's about saying how you feel *and* owning your own feelings."

He cocked his head. *"Go on."*

"Well, for example, instead of saying, 'It's all your fault, you did this and it made me mad,' people need to own it and say, 'When you did this, I got mad.' Or, 'When this happened, I was upset.' Sometimes it's called using 'I' words. They need to use the word 'I' so they take responsibility for their own upset. That way the other person won't be defensive, because you're not talking about them, you're talking about you, and your feelings only. Then they can actually hear you and it works out much better."

He smiled. *"Well said. I completely agree. Good job."*

Obviously considering the matter complete, he leaned back in his chair and closed his eyes, settling in for a nap or meditation; Kellie wasn't sure which. After a moment, she smiled slightly and leaned back herself, relaxing into the chair as she soaked in the beauty of the wild ocean with its white-capped waves.

An hour went by. The bright semicircle of radiant sun was just emerging over the rock archway when Laurie returned.

"I'm feeling better now," she said sincerely, sitting down in her chair and untying her running shoes. She slipped them off her feet one at a time, stripping off her socks as well and then burying her painted red toenails in the sand. The other two waited patiently. She studied her toes, wiggling them out of the sand and then burying them again. "It felt good to finally let it out. As for the destiny part, my life makes so much more sense now, even though I'm still trying to absorb it all."

She smoothed the sand all around her feet, evening it out until it was perfectly flat. "You said my grandfather died when it was his time to go, and that it had been planned for sixty years that he would die at that age. Is there such a thing as a pre-planned death date, or death year, for everyone?" she asked. "How does all of that work?"

"There's not a predestined death date or a precise moment that somebody is supposed to die. It's not like that.

But yes, it is predestined as to what age somebody will live to."

"All right. Let's just say that Grandpa was supposed to die at age sixty-four. If there's no specific day, why did he have to die the day after I said, 'Why don't you take somebody from my family,' as opposed to a week later, or a month later, or whatever?"

"*Well, first of all, if he had died earlier, then you wouldn't have said it,*" he said reasonably. "*Secondly, believe it or not, his day and time of death had absolutely nothing to do with what you had said a day earlier. It had everything to do with it being the perfect time for him to depart. Finally, your soul chose for you to say that exact thing at that exact time, because you were meant to be angry with me. It was an opportunity to set in motion the destiny card your soul had chosen to spread my word.*"

He angled his beach chair a bit more to the side, so he could stretch his legs out full length on the sand. "*Here's what I want you to know about death: It's never an accident. It only appears to be accidental, but it's not. There are predestined death windows, which are not so precise as to be to the day or the minute. Windows could be anywhere from a few days to a year. People often have multiple death windows preplanned into their lives. You might have just one window and that's it, or you might have two or three windows when you could choose to go. You all chose those windows before you were even born.*"

Bored with digging her toes in the smoothed-out sand, Laurie had progressed to burying her feet, which were now covered up to her ankles. "Why do some people have multiple windows?"

He locked his hands and put them behind his head,

gazing out at the peaceful ocean. *"Because things don't always work out the way you expect once you're here. It's like having a 'maybe' clause. Sometimes people want to go sooner, other times they want to take the last possible window. Please understand that it's not what you would consider a conscious choice. I don't want you getting mad at Aunt Emma because she chose to leave her three young kids, for instance. It's more of a deep-down, soul type of choice."*

He turned away from the ocean to look at Laurie. *"If you have a death window opening up, and you truly want to go, I'll help you—but only if you have a window. On the other hand, if you truly want to continue to live and not take the window, I'll help you do that as well."*

"What if you truly want to go, and you don't have a death window?" Kellie asked.

"Good question," he said. *"If you* don't *have a window available, then you're not meant to go at that time. There are bigger things going on. I'll say that again because I want to make sure it sinks in: There are times when people feel as though to go on living would be unbearable, but they aren't meant to go yet, for very good reasons."*

He looked pointedly at Kellie. *"For instance, so often you may not know it, but your mission is to be able to inspire others down the road who are experiencing difficult obstacles. Obstacles that you've overcome. So, of course, you have to stick around and get through those obstacles yourself first."*

"Boy, I can relate to that," Kellie said with feeling. "I remember when I was so, so sick during those ten years in bed. There were times I felt so horrible I just wanted to die. I remember just trying to get through an hour, one minute at a time. I couldn't even think about the next fifty-nine minutes or I wouldn't have been able to take it. Now, of course, I'm grateful I got through it. Obviously, I was meant to, so I could help others. But I'll tell you, if I'd had a death window then—"

"—*you would have taken it*," he finished for her. "*And that's exactly why you didn't have one. You're right, you were meant to live so you could inspire others one day.*"

CHAPTER 26

"What about *how* we die?" Kellie asked thoughtfully. "Do we decide that before we come into a life as well?"

He shook his head. "*You don't usually choose to die in a particular way. The death windows are the only thing that's preset, not the method of how you'll go.*"

Kellie reached down and began running sand idly through her fingers. "But what about when people get terminal illnesses like cancer? If they chose before they came in to get the illness, isn't that the same as choosing how you're going to die?"

"*That's tricky. Hmm . . . how can I explain this? Give me a moment.*"

He got up, walking down toward the waves. He rubbed his chin, contemplating as he gazed out at the ocean. Then he came back, moved his beach chair out of the way, and sat down cross-legged on the sand.

He snapped his fingers, and a deck of cards appeared in his left hand. "*You see, before you come in and begin your life, you decide on what cards you're going to get for your game. For instance, you might choose cancer,*" he held up one of the cards for them to see. "*You might also choose poverty, winning the lottery, having three kids . . .*"

He pulled a different card for each item and held them up, one at a time. "*You get the idea. But you don't know when and where those cards will come into play.*" He laid each card down randomly onto the sand, some in front of him, some to the side. "*You don't get to plan it out in that much detail. If you did, then it wouldn't be a game. It wouldn't be any fun. It's never meant to happen at a certain time; it's just supposed to happen at* some *time.*"

He picked up the cancer card and held it up. "*Getting an illness is a soul card. So you might choose to get cancer or a different illness for the lessons it provides you, and sometimes even for the lessons it provides those around you as well. It may help you appreciate and love things more, for instance. But it happens randomly. Let's say you get cancer as a ten-year-old, and your first death window isn't until you're fifty-eight. There's no way you'll die. But if you get it when you're fifty-seven, then yes, you'll most likely die of it within a year.*"

Kellie bent down and picked up the "three kids" card, considering it. "Wow, this stuff is a lot more complicated than I would have thought!"

"*It's an intricate game,*" he agreed. "*Essentially, even though you might get an illness, you chose the illness, but you didn't necessarily choose to die from it. Also, just so you know, as a soul, when you made that choice, you were probably confident you could easily conquer the challenge of that illness.*"

Laurie reached down and picked up a card, comparing it to the others in the sand. "Does that mean you can always recover from any illness, even cancer?"

He was silent, apparently thinking. Then he answered slowly, "*I want to say yes, because it is possible. But the majority of humans haven't advanced far enough yet to be able to count on doing that. It can be very, very challenging. However, if a person has more death windows in their future available and doesn't want to take the one that's currently open, there* are *those who beat the odds. People often say I performed a miracle, but I usually didn't. I meet you halfway; that's it. So if Bob beats the odds, he's the one who performed the miracle, not me. Give him the credit.*"

That caught Laurie's full attention. She put the card down and sat up straight. "So how do we beat the odds?"

He set the stack of cards that were left down in the sand. "*To beat the odds, you have to have something about you that keeps you living. Something like, 'I'm going to make it no matter what,' or, 'There's no way I'm leaving my child.' And, look for and eliminate any hidden beliefs that might sabotage you, such as, 'This cancer kills everybody.' That's a common one.*"

Laurie relaxed again. She picked up the stack he had set down and began idly shuffling the cards. "Well, if that's all we have to do, it seems as though more people would survive serious illnesses."

He sighed. "*As I said, it's extremely challenging. I don't want you blaming someone you love for dying because they didn't do what they were supposed to do in order to live. It's just not that easy for humans at this stage of your evolution. But what you always, always have the most control over is how you* respond *to the illness, don't forget that. And I'll tell you this as well: The negative things usually happen when you're unhappy, unfulfilled, discontented, and disgruntled.*

When you focus on negative thoughts, that's when your negative soul cards usually come into play."

Kellie eyed the gentle mounds of sand surrounding them, considering if she wanted to get up and walk back and forth in it. Making up her mind, she began taking off her shoes. "So if we work on remaining positive and only having positive thoughts, does that mean that our negative cards might never come into play?"

He tilted his head, considering. *"Since your soul chose the card, it will still be played eventually. However, there are some cards that could have a bigger or a smaller impact, depending on how the game goes. Not all of them, mind you. Some cards are simply non-negotiable because your soul wants that exact experience. But with others, your soul wants the option to lessen the impact. Your inner thoughts have an extraordinary amount of influence over your lives. They have control over what happens to you and when, and how you'll be impacted. And you are the one who chooses what those inner thoughts are going to be. So if you choose positive thoughts, then yes, with some cards you can lessen the impact."*

"Now hold on just a minute," Laurie said. "I specifically asked you when we first began this work if there was a way to lessen the impact and not have it be as bad, and you said no. Now you're changing your story. What's up with that?"

He looked at her calmly. *"At the time we were having that discussion, neither one of you understood or accepted that you had certain cards because your souls wanted those exact experiences. If I had told you then that you could lessen or change some of them, you wouldn't have understood what I wanted you to get, the way I wanted you to get it. You would never have accepted the cards that couldn't be changed. I wanted you to completely accept and be at peace with that critical part of the game first.*"

Laurie frowned. Then she said reluctantly, "You're right. I never would have accepted it as long as I thought it shouldn't be so bad. And I would have continued to be angry about the times when it did seem to be so bad, because I would just have kept thinking it didn't have to be, and that it was your fault for allowing it. Now I understand our souls better, and I see it differently."

He spread his hands out, palms up. "*So you see, when I say now that some cards can be lessened, and some can't, you're hearing it differently than you would have before.*"

He picked up a stick lying nearby and used it to draw in the sand. "*Let's go back to death windows, and how you can control whether or not you make your exit during one. Suppose you have a death window, but you don't want to take it. Imagine there's a certain amount of time between when you get sick and when you may die, or when you get into an accident and may die.*"

He had drawn two lines in the sand, one short and one long. "*Whether that amount of time is sixty seconds,*" he pointed at the short interval. "*Or six years,*" he pointed at the long interval. "*Your inner emotions, ideas, thoughts, and beliefs play a huge role in whether you live or die,*" he pointed at Laurie's chest. "*A huge role. How you look at things, what goes on inside of you, how you really and truly feel—all those things matter so much more than most people realize.*"

He set the stick down. "*So many of you feel unhappy, and I want to help you to get to the happy spot. I'm hoping this book you are going to write will help a lot of people get better at it. The key is to become aware of what goes on inside of you, and then to take control of it."*

Kellie had stopped her slow pacing. Walking in sand took too much effort. She gazed out at the sunlight glinting off the ocean. "You know, I think I'm really starting to get in my bones how much our thoughts determine how we live—or die, as the case may be."

She turned to look at him. "But then what, or who, ultimately decides *how* we die? Is it you?"

CHAPTER 27

"*W*ell, yes," he said slowly. "*I do make the final decision on when and how to take someone during a death window. But you need to understand there's a whole lot that goes into that decision. It's no small thing.*"

He paused, deep in thought. Eventually he said, "*Laurie, do you mind if I use your brother's fiancée and that whole incident as an example?*"

Laurie took a moment to reflect. "No, it's okay, go ahead. If it will help people understand, I know my brother and I'm sure he won't mind."

He got up, dusted the sand off his hands, grabbed the back of his beach chair and set it down directly facing the two women. He sat down, leaning forward intently. "*All right. Before I begin, I want you to prepare yourself to look at this example from the perspective of the soul. Remember, the soul sees things very differently. If you try to look at it from the perspective of a human, you might find yourself upset or offended. Which is perfectly okay, but it would be more helpful for you to understand it from the soul's point of view.*"

He reached down and idly picked up a handful of sand, then watched it run through his fingers as he considered his next words. "*I also want to make sure you absorb it in context. Please don't go out and try and explain how this works to anyone who doesn't have the understanding you've achieved with this work, or to anyone who is grieving the loss of a loved one. It will likely not comfort them in their pain and could very well make them feel worse. This example is for those who have learned enough about the soul's perspective to understand it* from *that perspective.*"

He leaned back in his chair, folded his hands in his lap and looked at them with a serious expression. "*Recently, Laurie's brother's fiancée and her sister were killed in a car accident,*" he said quietly. "*They were hit by a semi-truck in the middle of an intersection. I want to make sure it's perfectly clear that this was purely an accident—at least from a human perspective. From the higher perspective of the soul, one of the women was going to die from an illness within a year anyway, and she had an open death window. The other woman was incredibly pissed off at the world; she was done with it.*

She wanted *me to take her, and she also had a death window.*"

The deck of cards was still sitting on the sand. He leaned forward and picked up a card from the top, holding it out between his fingers. "*The driver of the semi-truck had a soul card that he was going to kill some people. Exactly how and when that would happen hadn't been determined yet.*"

Choosing his words carefully, he said, "*It just so happened that, from the perspective of their souls—did you catch that?*" They both nodded, and he repeated it for emphasis: "*From the perspective of their souls, this was a fabulous opportunity for everyone involved: The woman who was ill had not chosen a soul card that necessitated a lingering or painful death, so this was a chance to avoid that and just go quickly. The woman who was pissed off had a chance to get her wish and have me take her. And the driver of the semi had a chance to play his soul card in a situation that was purely an accident."*

Once again, he leaned back in his chair. *"Now, from a human perspective, I know this seemed like a horrible, horrible tragedy. But can you see how it was from a soul perspective? And can you see how everything had to fall into place for each individual involved, in order for things to happen the way they did? All of their karma and soul cards, their decisions and their death windows lined up perfectly, so I gave the 'okay' for it to happen. Again, I always have the final say."*

"So," Laurie said, "Even though my brother was devastated, and of course I would never have said this to him, from the point of view of all of their souls it was really a blessing in disguise."

"It was," he agreed. *"And just so you know, losing someone he loved and adored so he could learn to make it without her was one of the soul cards your brother's soul chose. Quickly was best for him, too. A long, drawn-out death would have been even harder for him to deal with."*

Using his hands to express himself and make his point, he said, *"Everyone the incident affects matters. How they will respond to the death always comes into play. What do they want to experience? What are their personal soul cards? What are the plans of all the souls that are touched by the death? The ripples are endless, truly. And once again, do* not *say this to someone who is grieving, but everything happens for a reason. It was meant to happen. There are no accidents, not ever. And take note, I allow these things only if all the souls involved are in agreement.*"

He stopped and dropped his hands in his lap again. The sound of ocean waves crashing on the shore was all that broke the silence, as both women, wide-eyed, absorbed the information.

After a while, Laurie spoke: "What about murder? You can't always keep people from flying off the handle, using their free will and killing somebody else, can you?"

He looked at her gravely. "*Murder is never random, even though it may look that way. Just like the incident I described involving Laurie's brother, there are many, many people who will be affected. So when it comes to murder, the one who does the murdering, the one who gets murdered, the mothers and fathers, spouses, friends, everyone who will be affected, all of their souls were in on the planning and have complimentary cards. All chose to experience the murder in whatever role they assumed. It's all prearranged, for the experiences and lessons it provides everyone involved.*"

"Is there a difference between accidentally killing someone and purposely killing them?" Kellie asked. "And what about deliberately planning it versus in the heat of the moment?"

"*There are cards that are specifically accidental, cards that are premeditated, cards that are 'in the heat of the moment,' and cards that could go one way or another, depending on how the game goes. Some offer the soul more choices in how it happens than others. There are cards where the person kills to protect someone they love. There are cards where they kill someone as a soldier in war.*

"*But don't make any assumptions. Even when it's*

premeditated, it doesn't always mean you're the bad guy. You might be the policeman or FBI agent who plans to kill someone who's been killing a lot of other people. An accidental card is not always better either. You might be robbing a store and accidentally kill the store owner or his son."

"But 'Thou Shalt Not Kill' is the biggest of the Ten Commandments," Laurie protested. "Why do you have cards for and prearrange something that goes against what you yourself have said not to do?"

Once again choosing his words carefully, he said, *"Before I set down the Ten Commandments, killing was considered a fun game. Combatants were pitted against each other, killing each other all the time for sport. People were betting on it, Kings were watching for entertainment, and no one thought there was anything wrong with it."*

He looked at them with a very serious expression. *"It really is not right to hurt another human being. But, to expand your soul, you all go through different experiences in different lifetimes, including doing things that are not right. That's how you grow as a soul. Everyone has to be the bad guy, and everyone has to be the victim. If there were no rules to break, how could you experience being the bad guy or the victim?*

"It's how you respond that matters. Are you going to be defiant and think, 'No one treats me like that!' Do you feel like the winner? Do you initiate a riot? Or do you feel remorseful and regret it? Do you apologize to the family?

"There are all kinds of moral dilemmas that can only be understood by you (and your soul) once you wrestle with them. It might be your job in the army when you're at war to kill people. How will you handle that? Maybe

you're defending your country. How do you reconcile that within yourself? The same is true for the other rules or Commandments. Even though you know it's wrong, maybe you have to steal to feed your starving family. How will you reconcile that?

"Human beings need to have rules. You must know what you're not supposed to do. Rules are part of the game. Humans do things they're not supposed to do. Just like children when you tell them they can't have a cookie until after dinner. Sometimes they sneak a cookie anyway. When you do things you're not supposed to, you experience and learn from the consequences. You acquire wisdom. Souls crave experience, and they crave wisdom, to be perfectly whole and complete."

He looked at Laurie. *"Do you understand?"*

She nodded slowly. "I think so. We could probably talk about this for days, but I think I understand the essence of it."

He turned and looked at Kellie. She gave a long, drawn-out sigh. "Yeah, I understand."

Still contemplating the information, she stood up and stretched.

"That looks like a good idea," Laurie said, standing up and stretching as well. "I like that we came to the beach. The peacefulness of the waves crashing is helping me stay calm through all of these sensitive subjects."

"Me too," Kellie agreed. "I still have more questions though. Not about murder, but about death."

He gave her a nod. *"I'm not going anywhere. That's my only job right now, to answer your questions. Go ahead."*

CHAPTER 28

Kellie hesitated. "Well, this might be kind of a touchy subject for some people."

"*Touchier than murder?*"

"Uh, good point. Okay. What about suicide? Is that a soul card? Is it preplanned?"

His features became stern. The two women unconsciously sat up a bit straighter.

"*Suicide is not a soul card,*" he said, "*and it is never preplanned. It is never supposed to happen, never. I know that appears to contradict what I've said about the soul needing to experience every single thing in order to be complete, but suicide is the* one *exception. I want to be very clear about this from the start: Harming yourself is not an experience you are ever meant to have. You have enough to deal with without that. It pains me terribly when humans decide to take their own lives. I do not approve at all.*

"*Before I go into it anymore, though, I want to say that many people who talk about killing themselves don't really intend to. They are just reaching out for help. So take it as a serious cry for help, and do whatever you can for them. Suicide is really trying to take the easy way out. You don't learn your lesson; you don't even attempt to. It's like you're opting out, you're quitting, and you're not even trying.*

"And you're ruining not only your own game, but everyone else's as well. For instance, some people get sick and don't want to put others around them through the aggravation of caring for them. They don't realize that those others have chosen to support someone in need. Whether you're an aggravation or not, those people have a game piece they've chosen, as a soul, to help someone in serious need. You're taking away their game as well as yours.

"When you kill yourself, I'm not going to pat you on the back and be sympathetic. I'm going to have a very serious talk with you about the situation. I'll show you how you could have handled it a different way. I'll help you understand how you could have stayed and succeeded.

"I'll send you back to watch how your death affects everyone. You'll have to witness the pain you caused them, and it's severe. When you kill yourself, you are hurting so many other humans. They have so many unanswered questions: 'Why? What was he thinking? How could she have done this?' It's painful, because they aren't able to get answers. To watch them is horrible, because you see how much torture you put everyone through. You also see how much you actually were cared for. You realize that you really were loved.

"Some don't have any family. But they still go back and see how it affected people. It might be their next-door neighbor, who always appreciated how nice and considerate they were. It might be the people at the grocery store, who enjoyed them because they always had a smile or a joke to offer. No matter what, every person who opts for suicide regrets it afterward.

"There is always an answer, a way out. If there weren't, you would have a death window. If there's no death window, there's a way out. You're meant to stay. It's that simple. Your soul is strong, ferocious, and brave. As a soul, you chose a horrendous situation because you knew you could handle it. You knew you could get yourself out of it. You knew you could find a way out. Sometimes it's tough and you can't see it, but it's there." He leaned forward, looking at them intently with those piercing eyes of his. *"I want the whole world to hear this,"* he commanded. *"There is* always *a way out.*

"Ask me for help. Call on me when it gets bad. I do help. You must *keep going. Killing yourself is not one of your options. If you do kill yourself, I'm going to send you right back to start all over again with another life, right back into the same situation again and say, 'Figure it out. How else can you handle it? What other decisions can you make?' You're going to have to go back and do it all over again anyway, so you may as well figure it out the first time. I'll send you back as many times as you need to make the right decision, but why put yourself through all of that again?*

"I know you suffer. But in your darkest hour, remember, if you make the wrong decision, you'll be going back to earth to play that same game again and again until you get it right.

"Now, I'm not quite as hard on the children who kill themselves. I feel worse for them. They don't have the wisdom and the experience the adults do. But in the end, it's no different. They still have to go back again into the same situation and figure it out.

"The purpose of the entire game of life is for you to make yourself happier and feel better. It's not to quit or to

lose. It's for you to uplift yourself and feel more complete. I don't know how much more clearly I can say, 'Don't do it—there is always a way out.'"

Once again, the rhythm of the waves pounding on the sandy beach was the only sound that disturbed the poignant silence.

After what seemed an eternity, Kellie took a deep breath and asked her last question:

"What about huge disasters, like Hurricane Katrina and 9/11? Does every single person who dies have a death window? Are those things always orchestrated and planned as well?"

Laurie, who had been staring out at the ocean, snapped her head around. "Oh, I definitely want to know the answer to that one, too."

"Well, that's a bit different than anything we've talked about so far. Most people who die in a big disaster have a soul card to do that. 'I'm going to die in a huge disaster' is a card they play, even though it's not planned beforehand when and where, and even if they don't have a death window just then.

"There are a few exceptions like that. Another exception is 'I'm going to die for my country.' It could be in the service, but it also could be in something like the terrorist attack on 9/11, or even in the airplane stopping the 9/11 terrorists from bombing the White House.

"If it's a soul card, there are a few exceptions like these that can happen whenever, regardless of when the individual's death windows are. Another possible exception is, 'I will give my life for someone, if need be.' That card could be combined with a death window, or not, depending on what the soul chose before coming in."

"You know, the more I learn from you, the more everything really does sound just like a game," Kellie said. "A very real, very in-your-face, no-holds-barred kind of game, for sure. But it is, essentially, a game."

"*It's the soul's game,*" he agreed. "*It's the game of life. When you die, it's actually a relief, even when it's a sudden death. Those of you left behind think it's the most horrible thing. People get so upset when entire families go, and that upset is perfectly understandable. But from the soul's perspective, it's actually the greatest thing ever. They all get to go together! It's actually quite pleasant and enjoyable. It's really just a transitional time, the end of the game of life. I know you here on earth miss them terribly. I understand the sadness. But death is just a part of life.*"

He leaned forward, looking at them each in turn, an expression of sincerity on his face and also in his tone.

"*I'd love it if you celebrated someone's life after their death, instead of mourning them. Celebrate their death as a celebration of life! If you humans could just think back and celebrate all that person brought into the world, it would uplift you. Think of how they inspired you, how they motivated you.*

"*If you could remember how he inspired you and carry that fire he lit up within you, instead of crying about losing him, it would be so wonderful and so powerful. Try asking yourself, 'How can I be lit up by her today? What did she say that she would want me to carry around with me? How could she empower my day?'*"

He sat back and smiled. "*And you know what? Not only would it light up* your *day, but from where your loved ones are now, it would light up theirs as well, to see you happy and inspired as you carry them around in your heart. It would make them so happy to see you joyfully living your life to the fullest."*

And on that note, still smiling, he stood up. *"I think that's enough for today. I've given you a lot to think about."* Then, shark swimsuit whipping against his legs in the afternoon wind, gray-streaked brown hair flying wildly around his head, he strode back into the ocean, disappearing into the foamy green waves.

PART VI

HEAVEN

CHAPTER 29

Santa Cruz, California

"I wonder why everywhere we meet God is in the United States," Kellie said idly.

She and Laurie were sitting on the bumpy meadow grass high up on the bluff near her house, looking out over Santa Cruz. It was the day after their interaction at the beach with the old man. They could see the ocean in the distance, and the orange sun was sinking slowly down toward the mountains on their left. The pink-tinged clouds were promising a beautiful sunset.

"Just 'cause we live here, I guess," Laurie said.

"*Actually, it's mostly because of the time difference,*" boomed a familiar voice.

They looked around but didn't see him anywhere. "Where are you?" Kellie asked, caught off balance.

"*Never mind,*" he replied. "*Would you like a special treat?*"

"Sure," both women chorused.

"After yesterday's topic at the beach, I think we could use one," Laurie said candidly.

"Okay, but you're going to have to wake up and be ready to go in the middle of the night. Are you ladies up for that?"

"Sounds like an adventure to me," Kellie said with excitement. "I'm game. "

Laurie?"

"You bet! What time?"

"Two a.m. sharp. Just walk out your front door and you'll know where to go," he said mysteriously.

"What should we wear?" Laurie asked, always eager to dress appropriately for the occasion.

But the only answer was the sound of the wind blowing steadily across the bluff.

"Ouch!" Right hand on the railing, Kellie reached out with her left to steady Laurie, who had run into her on the stairs in the dark.

"Shhhh," Laurie whispered. "We don't want to wake up Brett and the boys, right?"

"No, of course not, but kindly try not to step on me, okay? I don't want to turn the light on, because even that might wake them up, and for sure Tessa will wake up and want to come with us."

"Will she bark?"

"I hope not. Just follow me."

Laurie followed her as she wove her way among the dim shapes of the couches and coffee tables, taking care not to trip over any of the many beautiful houseplants situated along the length of the picture window.

"Be careful not to let Leia slip out the front door," Kellie whispered. "She's sleeping on the cat tower over there, but she's quick, and as an indoor cat I'd prefer she stay safely inside."

They had decided to dress casually, but nicely. When they finally reached the front door, Kellie unlocked and opened it slowly, peering out into the front yard. It looked perfectly normal. "What did he say when you called him in?"

"He said to go out the front door and we'd see the doorway. Once we're on the other side, we're supposed to make sure we're on New Street," Laurie said helpfully.

"Okay, c'mon." As soon as they stepped out and Kellie closed the door softly, the familiar hum—and then the doorway—appeared to the right of the porch, shimmering in mid-air.

"Oh no," Laurie said in dismay. "We're going to have to jump!"

"It'll be fun," Kellie said encouragingly. "Come on, I'll go first."

One at a time, they jumped through the doorway and landed on a cement sidewalk in broad daylight. Looking around, they squinted and blinked in the bright sun, trying to get oriented. Kellie saw the sign that said, "New Street." They seemed to be in some kind of market district, with shops ranging up and down each side of the street.

She did a 360-degree turn and saw they were standing directly in front of a shop with large, beautiful archway windows. Etched in white on the glass was a bowl with a spoon in it, a halo around the top of the bowl and angel wings on either side. Under the bowl and between the wings it said, "A Slice of Heaven." There was a white wrought-iron table and chairs on the sidewalk in front of the shop.

"Look!" Laurie exclaimed.

Kellie peered into the shop and there he was, sitting at an inside table, beckoning them in. He was dressed entirely in green, from a sparkly green hat to sparkly green shoes, with green breeches and waistcoat in between. In fact, he looked remarkably like a very large leprechaun.

"Oh, no," Kellie groaned. She started to turn around to leave.

Laurie grasped her shoulders firmly, pointed her back toward the door to the shop, and gave her a shove. "There's no escape now. C'mon, let's go."

As they moved toward the door, a gentleman who was on his way out held it open for them, tipping his hat as they thanked him. They walked hesitantly into the cool interior.

Their eyes adjusted to the dim light, widening as they saw a glass case with all kinds of tempting desserts behind it. There was an antique framed mirror on one wall of the large room, and the other walls were covered in antique-looking wallpaper, with ornately framed pictures hanging majestically here and there. Small tables and chairs were scattered strategically about, with patrons sitting in front of some of the most beautiful and mouth-watering confections Kellie had ever seen.

She glanced sideways at the old man. "Do we have to let on that we know him?" she said to Laurie out of the side of her mouth. "I can't believe he's dressed like that! How embarrassing. Maybe we can sit at a different table?"

Laurie laughed. "He'd probably just get up and come join us. Hey, you know what? Listen to the server speaking to that customer up there who's ordering. Guess where I think we are?"

Kellie listened. Both women spoke with a lovely lilting

Irish brogue. She looked at Laurie, wide-eyed. "Oh, my God! Do you think we're in *Ireland?*"

"Yup, I do." Laurie gave a nod toward the old man in his green finery. "Hence the ridiculous leprechaun outfit."

A few of the customers waiting in line were staring curiously at the old man. He seemed oblivious, carefully studying a small menu that read "A Slice of Heaven Dessert Café" on the cover. He glanced up, then beckoned them toward him again.

They looked at each other with undisguised dismay, then reluctantly shuffled over to the table and sat down with him, carefully not looking up at any of the other patrons.

"Really?" Kellie snatched the menu out of his hands and buried her nose in it. Her slightly muffled voice rose from the depths of the menu as she continued, "Did you have to dress like that?"

"Like what?"

She made a guttural noise of exasperation. "Right. Never mind. Ooooo, Laurie, look at this menu!" Embarrassment forgotten for the moment, she leaned over, showing Laurie the menu and pointing to the cheesecake section. "Caramel Crunch, Turkish Delight, Totally Toblerone—mmmmm!"

"Ooooo—look over here," Laurie pointed with enthusiasm. "Cheeky Chocolate Fudge Cake and Tantalising Tiramisu!"

"Go ahead and order whatever you like," he said. *"I know the owner, so it's on the house."*

Giggling and oooo-ing and ahhh-ing like little girls promised a birthday treat, they had almost as much fun deciding what to order as they did actually eating the scrumptious desserts.

Kellie slowly finished the last bite of her milk chocolate and honeycomb cheesecake, reluctantly pushed the plate away, and sank back in the straight-backed chair. "Thank you," she said sincerely. "That was, well, truly heavenly!"

Laurie agreed wholeheartedly. "Yes, it certainly was. Thank you."

"*You're welcome,*" he said graciously. "*Both of you deserved a treat. You've been working very hard gathering the information in our sessions, and it hasn't always been easy for either one of you. Ready to begin?*"

"Yes," Kellie said. "Based on our treat, you obviously know what we're going to ask about today, so I'll just dive right in. You've talked a lot about the game of life we play down here on earth. Well, what other games do we play? What do we do when we die and go to heaven and are in spirit or soul form? I'm sure we don't just sit around in heaven and say, 'Whoo-hoo! We're in heaven; how cool is this?' There are other games we play, right?"

He laughed. With a twinkle in his eye that was perfectly in character with his leprechaun persona, he replied, "*You know what? I always think it's nice to have people do that for a while. I encourage them to sit around in heaven and say, 'Whoo-hoo! I'm in heaven! How totally, completely, and unbelievably cool is this?' Some people enjoy that to no end. However, some people are at a loss when they don't have anything specific to do. So I give them something to do. When you're in that spiritual realm, you get to feel good, feel proud, and feel satisfied. So I make sure you're happy and you get quite a bit of say-so in what you want to do.*"

"Sounds great," Laurie said enthusiastically. "Yeah," Kellie echoed. "Tell us more!"

CHAPTER 30

"*There are all kinds of worlds up there,*" the old man began. "*You get to make some choices when you pass on. Many of you choose to stay close to earth to watch your loved ones, which is fine. Some of you opt to do certain specific jobs. I don't enforce whether you have to do this or do that. But I certainly will help you choose and influence you in the direction I think would benefit you.*"

"What kind of jobs are there?" Kellie asked curiously.

"*The games, the jobs, up here are difficult to describe because you have no context for many of them. Fifty years ago, before computers, if you tried to explain to someone what it's like to invent software, they would have looked at you with a blank stare. They just wouldn't have been able to comprehend what you were talking about. That's what a lot of the jobs are like up here. It's too hard to put it into concepts you would understand.*"

Kellie frowned. "Do they have anything to do with helping people on earth, or are they completely removed from life here?"

"*A lot of them have to do with the earth and with the humans on earth. Some have to do with the plants on earth.*"

Some have to do with the animals on earth. Some have to do with things in the heavenly realm. Some have to do with thought processes. There are a multitude of jobs to do, and you can opt to do any of them you like when you pass on."

Laurie leaned forward eagerly. She had softened toward the old man since releasing her anger toward him on the beach. "Can you tell us about one that we might understand a bit more than the others?"

Appearing to enjoy Laurie's new attitude, he leaned forward as well, hands clasped in front of him on the table. *"One job someone might choose would be to tend to the animals. The spiritual animals, that is, the deceased ones."*

She looked puzzled. "You mean they still need to be taken care of?"

He knitted his brows. *"Well, it's not like being down on earth where they have to be washed and fed and watered. It's not physical. It's more of an interaction thing. The human spirits interact with the animal spirits."*

"So the animals need to be interacted with."

"No," he said slowly, it's actually the other way around. It's more that the human spirits need to interact with the animals."

Her puzzled features relaxed. "Oh, I see."

He smiled. *"It's a wonderful thing up here. More so even than on earth, because for some people, it is their greatest love to have their cats or their dogs. So just think, when you die and come up to heaven, what would be the most fun thing you could do? For some people, it's taking care of their favorite pets. There's no judgment. You can take care of a ton of cats and not be called a 'cat lady' and made fun of, like you might here on earth. So those lovely animals are more for your entertainment than anything else."*

"Do pets reincarnate like people do?" Kellie asked.

He nodded. *"Yes, animals reincarnate. You could actually get a pet with a little doggy, kitty, gerbil or whatever soul when you're a child, then get another pet with that same little animal soul again when you're an old grandma, too. It doesn't even have to be that long. They're really just like humans. They come up to heaven, stay a while, and then come back down again. They don't get to stay up here. I don't care if you're the best dog or the best kitty-cat or the best horse or whatever. You're always going to go back down, sooner or later."*

"Do humans ever reincarnate as animals, or vice-versa?" Laurie asked.

"No. Animal souls are different. Humans only reincarnate as humans."

Being the animal lover she was, Kellie's curiosity kicked into high gear: "Then what is their purpose? Are they learning lessons? Are they doing jobs? Are they playing games?"

He laughed. *"Whoa! Slow down. No, not like the humans. They're really just here for you. Think: What brings great joy to a human? An animal. It doesn't necessarily have to be a pet that snuggles up with you on the couch. It could be the animal you've watched at Sea World. It could be the animal you see on the animal channel. Animals bring curiosity and wonder."*

"And they keep coming back to the humans they love in different forms?"

He shrugged. *"Sometimes yes, and sometimes no."*
"Who decides?"
"I do."
"So why can't we always have the same beloved pet soul come back to us?"

He pondered for a moment. *"Well, you might think it would be a nice thing to have the same soul as your pet again, but consider this: Do you really want the same dog personality over and over and over again? I doubt it. That's why I don't always send the same one back."*

"What about in future lives or incarnations?" Kellie asked. "Do we connect with the same pet souls again in that case?"

"Not all the time, but often you do, yes, just like with people."

Suddenly a small boy appeared at the table, eyes as big as tea saucers as he looked at the old man. "Look Mammy, it's a Leprechaun!"

A middle-aged woman with ample curves stood behind him. "Come on Liam, we don't want to bother these people."

The old man smiled warmly at the little boy. *"Oh, no bother."* He leaned forward conspiratorially and whispered, *"Would you like to have a piece of real Leprechaun gold?"*

The boy's eyes grew even rounder. "Oh, yes!"

"Here you go." He held out his open hand, which was empty. He closed the hand into a fist, a single chime rang out, and when he opened it again, there was a shiny gold coin lying on his palm.

"Oooo!" the boy squealed, picking up the coin, and turning to his mother. "Look, Mammy! Can I keep it? Please?"

She looked questioningly at the old man, who nodded. "Yes," she said. "You may keep it. Say thank you."

The boy looked at the coin reverently. "Thank you, Mr. Leprechaun!"

"Okay, Liam, let's go, your daddy's waiting." She

smiled gratefully at the old man, took the boy by the hand, and left.

"What about me?" Kellie said, teasing. "Where's my Leprechaun gold?"

"*It wouldn't impress you nearly as much,*" he quipped.

She yawned and stretched. "You're right, of course. I think I need a cup of tea. It's 3:30 in the morning for us!"

"I'll get it," Laurie said. "I want one, too. Should I get a pot for all of us?"

He nodded. "*When you get back, I'll share one of the most awesome benefits of being in heaven that a lot of people don't even realize.*"

He smiled and winked at them mischievously. "*You're going to love it.*"

Laurie returned with the tea and filled three cups, leaving plenty of room for cream and sugar. She plopped down a stack of extra napkins for everyone, then sat down and adjusted her diabetic pump.

Once they had stirred in the goodies and begun sipping the sweet and creamy tea, Kellie gave a contented sigh. "Okay, that was a very tantalizing little tidbit you dropped on us before we took a break," she said. "Care to elaborate?"

"*I wanted to make sure you didn't fall asleep,*" he teased. "You succeeded. So . . . c'mon, give us the skinny!"

"*Okay. One of the greatest parts about being in heaven is that, when you're a spirit, you can be in quite a few different places at the exact same time. As a human in a body, you're used to being in only one place at a time. But as a spirit, you could be here listening to this conversation, you could be up playing with the spirit dogs, and you could*" *be hanging out in the oval office, checking out what the President is up to right now—all at the same time. And you'd be very peaceful, calm, and happy about it. How's that for solving your, 'There's just not enough time in the day' dilemma, huh? What do you two think of that?"*

"I'd like to be peaceful, calm, and happy any which way I could," Laurie said frankly.

"I think it sounds exciting," Kellie said enthusiastically. "Is that really true for everyone in heaven? They can be in different places and not get confused? And what about you? Is it true for you as well?"

"It's true for everyone in heaven, myself included. That is how I'm able to listen to and respond to so many at the same time. That should give you something else to look forward to."

Kellie held her palms up facing him. "It does, but not just yet, thanks. Unless my last death window has arrived, I'm not done with everything I want to do here on earth," she said, laughing.

CHAPTER 31

"This is all so interesting," Kellie continued, "but I'm wondering about all the people who write books because they think they know exactly what goes on after people die. They are so specific! For instance, 'Then you go into this room and guides speak to you, and then this happens, and then that happens.' Where do they get all that from?"

He pushed his chair out a bit and sat back, crossing his right leg over his left. *"There's at least a glimmer of truth in all of those books that are published, sometimes more than a glimmer. And just so you know, the ones who make it all up on purpose to try and make money, their books don't ever get published. Frankly, I'm not terribly concerned with the accuracy of the published books. What I like about them is that they take away fear and give people hope. I don't want you to be afraid of what happens after you die. So if the descriptions in those books comfort people, I'm happy. But I'll tell you right now, there's not one set way that you die, with your spirit going from this point to that point to another point. It's different for every soul."*

"Can you give us some examples?" Laurie asked.

"*Look into your teacups.*" They each picked up their cup and looked in at the remaining tea. Kellie saw it swirl as pictures of people began to form, depicting joyous reunions of all kinds.

"*Each soul's going to do it a little bit differently. Your guides are there to help sometimes. Yes, your dead mom, dad, grandma, grandpa, brother, sister, or dog is there to greet you sometimes. Yes, sometimes you go up to the light. Sometimes. Sometimes you just pop right over. Sometimes you find some pearly gates. Sometimes you don't. It's not as though, 'First you do this, then you do that, then you go through here.' It's different for everybody.*"

"What about hell and what about demons? Do they exist?" Laurie asked curiously.

Kellie hastily set her teacup back down on the table, just in case. She didn't want to see anything that would give her nightmares later.

He chuckled. "*Don't worry Kellie. There's no hell—and there's no devil. Demons? It depends on your definition of demons. There are certainly some humans out there who act demonic, and there are certainly some spirits out there who act demonic as well. But they're not all in this one place full of fire and brimstone, where you go if you've been a bad boy or a bad girl.*"

"But can they get you?" Laurie asked uncertainly. "Like in *Ghost*, the evil guys got torn up by the demons instead of going into the light. Was that just drama, or was there any truth to that?"

He shook his head emphatically. "*No, but they did make it look pretty good in that movie, didn't they?*"

They all laughed.

He put both feet on the floor and leaned forward again,

gently thumping his right hand on the table and holding it there for emphasis. "*It's not like that, because once again—and I keep repeating this because it's so important that you truly understand it—you're all beautiful, wonderful souls. You just choose a particular lifetime to do the bad, nasty things. No matter how it looks to you from a human perspective, there is no such thing as hell because there is no soul who is innately 'bad.' This may make some people angry, but even the most evil people in history were not innately bad.*"

"So we all always end up in heaven and in the light, no matter which way we get there?" Laurie pressed.

"*Yes,*" he said simply, and leaned back in his chair again.

She gave a sigh of relief. "That ought to take all the fear away from everybody."

He raised his eyebrows, lowered his head slightly and gave her a pointed look. "*I certainly hope so. That's how it should be. I don't want anyone to be afraid of passing on or dying, because there is nothing to be afraid of.*"

She smiled. "It actually sounds kind of fun—once you get there, I mean."

Kellie had noticed a pen lying on the floor and bent down to pick it up. She took one of the extra napkins off the stack and began idly doodling on it while she listened.

"Okay, I have another question," Laurie said.

He gestured toward her with his right hand, encouraging her to continue. "*Let's hear it.*"

She paused for a moment, then continued. "When people are up there in the light, you say they have jobs. Well, are there friendships and relationships there? Do they hang out with friends? Or is everybody just kind of into the light and into themselves?"

"It's different with different people. Some people do hang out with their family members: husbands, wives, even their pets. Some just do their jobs. It's very hard for me to explain why some would do some things and some would do others. What you need to understand is that when you're up here, all of the emotion that you have on earth is not readily available. I'll use Kellie and her boys as an example. Kellie, it isn't as though you would think: 'Oh, Kyle's here! Where's Aron? Wait, oh, no, this is terrible, I only get Kyle and not Aron!'"

Kellie flipped her napkin over and began doodling a picture of herself and of Kyle, adding angel wings to both of them.

"It might be that Kyle has chosen to just hang out and float around, and maybe Aron has moved on to be somebody's spirit guide. So you and Kyle might be hanging out, and even though Aron is a guide, every once in a while he'll pop in and say, 'Hey, Mom, Hey, bro.' And remember, he can also be in different places at the same time, which makes it even easier."

Now she grabbed another napkin and doodled a picture of Aron, with wings. "So Aron lives somewhere else and comes to visit, and Kyle lives with me, is it like that?"

"Kind of like that, yeah."

"Hmm." She moved the two napkins apart, then together. "You say the same emotions aren't readily available. I've always had the picture that your emotions all go away when you go to heaven and you just bliss out. But I've talked to my guides through Laurie, and I have one guide in particular who has gotten very angry about something. And it bothered me, not even so much what she was angry about, but the fact that she was so angry. I thought, 'wait a minute—how can she be angry? I don't understand. That's not a positive emotion. That's a negative emotion. How can that be?' So please tell me more about how emotions work when you're a spirit."

"Guides in particular are more privy to emotions, because, think about it, how effective would they be as a guide for humans if they didn't have emotions or feelings available to them? It just makes them more effective. And if you love your work and you have the emotion of feeling passionate about it, when you really love what you do, you do a better job. Do you understand?"

Above Kellie's doodle of herself, she drew a friendly-looking female angel with wings to represent her spirit guide, Jacqueline. "I think so. You actually decide whether emotions are available or not to spirits? You believe that guides are better off with them, so you allow guides to have them?"

He shrugged. *"Pretty much."* He held his right index finger up in the air. *"And I'd like to point out, for the record, that her anger was on your behalf."*

"That's true," Kellie said. "She was angry because of how someone treated me." She doodled a harp and some pearly gates next to the angel/guide. "So, people who aren't guides who are up in heaven don't have emotions?"

He shook his head. *"I'm not saying that. It's not that they don't have emotions at all. It's that the intensity of emotions isn't there. For instance, when you first pass on, if your emotions were the same you would certainly expect to feel sad watching your own funeral. But you don't, because you don't have emotions that would be detrimental to you."*

"Negative emotions, you mean."

He held up his right index finger again. *"I didn't say negative, I said emotions that would be detrimental to you."*

"Like sadness and anger and—"

He interrupted her. "*Anger is not always detrimental. Actually, sadness isn't either. I block only those emotions that would be detrimental to you in particular as the soul. For instance, one emotion might be just fine for one soul, but that exact same emotion would be detrimental to a different soul. So once again, it's a case-by-case thing. It's not like there's just one answer for every soul.*"

Kellie set her pen down. "Would you please define 'detrimental?'"

"*Something that would really hurt them, slow them down, that would keep them from enjoying their job, or enjoying their state of being. Not everybody has a job in heaven.*"

"I think I get it," Laurie said. "Their state of being is happiness, and anything that would prevent that is not there?"

"*Right. But you could have a little anger here and there. Which is fine; it doesn't hurt what you do.*"

"But people don't get depressed or bored in heaven, right?"

He shook his head emphatically. "*No, definitely not. No one ever gets depressed or bored in heaven, never ever.*"

There was a companionable silence as they all took a break and sipped their tea.

Kellie stifled a yawn. "Heaven sounds every bit as good as rumor has it, wouldn't you say so, Laurie?"

"Yes, I would. It sounds lovely."

The old man smiled at them. "*Heaven really is the beautiful place you hear about in fairy tales and stories. You get to name the game you play there. It's awesome. Think of it like this: Heaven is the grand prize for playing the 'human' game. It doesn't matter if you won or lost your*" *particular game. It doesn't matter if your game was horrible or delightful. As long as you played hard and stuck with it, you earned the reward. It's no different than when your child's soccer team plays hard in a tournament. Even if they lose, they still get to go out for ice cream afterward, because they stuck it out and did their best. So really, all you have to do to win the game of life and get the prize is to play."*

The smile faded, and his expression became serious again. *"The exception is if you take your own life and come too soon. That's like quitting the tournament without even trying. Heaven is not the almighty escape that will save you from the game you've chosen. Oh, you'll still get a couple of bites of ice cream, but that's it. You're only there for a moment; then you're right back in the game—the same game you thought you were getting out of. Everyone else gets to stay awhile, hang out with their buddies, and enjoy lots of ice cream. Make no mistake: You must play your game to get the reward."*

He slid his chair back, stood up and stretched. *"Have you two enjoyed your sweet reward for all of your hard work?"*

Laurie stood up as well. "Yes, thank you!"

Kellie picked up her napkins with the doodles and stuffed them in her pocket as a memento, then stood up. "Oh, yes, it was yummy. Thank you!"

He winked at them and nodded toward the front door of the sweet shop. "When you're ready, the doorway home will appear." Then, as he turned his back to walk away, in true leprechaun fashion, he jumped into the air and kicked his heels together with a sharp click. And then he strode out the door and was gone.

PART VII

HOW TO HAVE A NICE, HAPPY DAY

CHAPTER 32

Big Bear Lake, California

"I love that song about living your life the way you want to, instead of how other people think you should," Kellie said. She and Laurie were walking toward the car after seeing a local band play at The Cave in the Village at Big Bear Lake.

Just for fun, they had dressed up rock-n-roll style, loose flowing tops in their favorite colors and sparkling crystal studs on their jeans.

"Which one was that?"

"Don't you remember?" Kellie hummed a few bars. "It was the one where he just wasn't going to worry about what other people thought he should do. He was just going to do what made him happy—and in the last line in the chorus he told everyone else to do the same, and to have a nice day."

Kellie and her family had convinced Laurie to spend a few days on vacation with them at Big Bear Lake in Southern California before she had to return to Manhattan.

"Doing what makes you happy sounds like a great idea to me," Kellie continued, "As long as making yourself happy doesn't hurt anyone else, of course."

"Of course," Laurie said, then she stopped in her tracks. Kellie turned and looked at her. "What's up?"

"He's here," she said simply. "He says to call him in, because it's the perfect time to talk about—" she frowned, then her face cleared as she caught the words—"how to have a nice, happy day."

Kellie waited while Laurie surrounded them with the protective white light and called in God. She heard the familiar angelic chimes, felt a hand squeeze her shoulder, and turned around to see the old man standing there, grinning cheerfully at her.

He began walking, and they fell into step alongside him. *"Great concert, wasn't it?"* He was dressed like one of the band members, in a stylish black leather vest and black leather pants, with silver studs lining the outside of the pants legs. He wore a silver chain around his neck with a silver medallion that was engraved with "God, Games, and Rock 'n Roll."

"Yeah," Laurie said with enthusiasm. "They did a great job!"

They walked companionably along, the two women enjoying the afterglow from the concert while they waited for the old man to let them know how he wanted to proceed.

"Tonight," he began, *"I'm going to pick the topic. I want to talk about how to 'Have a nice, happy day.' So far I've talked about how to be happier in general, and tonight, I'd like to talk about how to have fun and be happy at any given moment in time."*

"Sounds good to me," Laurie said. "Where are we going?"

"How about we just walk around town for a bit?" he said.

"That sounds like a lovely idea." Kellie was feeling

lighthearted and actually skipped a step or two to catch up with them again.

"Yes, it does," Laurie agreed amiably.

They walked side-by-side, crossing the street and turning left, then right. The Village in Big Bear was beautiful even at night, designed with architectural highlights such as lovely red brick walkways, diamond-shaped red sidewalk slabs, and bright flowers of all colors splashed everywhere. The streetlamps were old-fashioned double lights with two large baskets of multicolored flowers springing from peat moss hanging under every light. It was late and everything was closed, so the sidewalks were empty.

"For many of you," he began, *"it's lack of energy, a lack of feeling good. It's feeling bad physically, feeling drained, feeling emotionally not up to par. You're too tired, physically and mentally. Do you ladies mind if we take a closer look at that?"*

"I think that's a great idea," Laurie said earnestly.

"Yeah, me too," Kellie agreed.

"Okay. I'd like to use you as an example, Laurie."

"Oh, great," she said drily.

"Actually, I'd like to use how you were ten years ago, before I first began speaking with you and Kellie. You've gotten much better, because you've been applying what you've learned. Kudos to you for that! So, do you mind if I talk about how you used to be? I'd like to, because what went on in your mind then is what goes on in many, many people's minds now."

"It's okay, I don't mind. Go ahead."

"Good. We'll start with a school day when Ben was five years old. Let's just go back in time and imagine you're sleeping, Laurie. The clock is about to go off in the morning.

You're going to wake up, and your train of thought will begin. Here we go: It's a constant litany of what's bad, what's wrong, what's negative. 'I don't want to get up . . . want to stay in bed . . . too tired . . . son's not doing what I want . . . this is such a hassle . . . wish I were back in bed . . . why doesn't he hurry up? Oh, we're going to be late . . . what a mess, oh no, watch the clock, hurry, hurry, hurry; let's go, let's go'.

"*Then, on the way to school: 'Never did fix that hole in the road . . . what is that guy doing crossing right in front of that truck? People are so rude . . . why do they expect everyone else to move out of their way? Ow, these shoes hurt my feet . . . I should have gotten the next size up . . .'*

"*I'm telling you exactly what used to go on in her mind. This is how everybody's mind works. Now, I'm going to tell you what came out of her mouth to Ben* at the very same time: '*What a lovely day . . . the sun is shining . . . let's run! Oh, let's balance on the rail . . . how's your teacher going to like your picture?' You should have seen her Skip to the Loo to school with her son. Her brain was going 'grouch, grouch, grouch,' and to her son she was a whole different personality. She had both going on at the exact same time!*"

Laurie had started laughing before he was done. "Yup, that sounds about right," she said, amused.

"She's always been very sweet to her son," Kellie commented.

"*I know. Laurie, I was picking on you because I knew you'd play the game with me, and because you've gotten so much better at just being happy. But for those of you reading this right now, you know you're exactly the same way as Laurie was. You may have a slightly different monologue going on, but it's the pretty much the same theme. If you think you're not the same, tune in. Tune in an hour from now, tune in tomorrow, and listen, listen to that inner voice. It is nonstop.*

"How difficult is that, to be having two conversations like so many of you do, with the real conversation going on in the back of your mind? Those negative conversations going on behind the scenes drain you, tire you, and take a horrible toll on you. Not just on your mind, but on your physical body. It's as though you're trying to stand up and someone's trying to pull you down at the same time. They are pulling, pulling, pulling hard, and it's putting a terrible strain on you."

He stopped at the corner, turned to face them, and put his hands on his hips as if daring them to contradict him.

CHAPTER 33

"*So, heck yeah, you're tired,*" the old man said. "*A whole lot of you are tired, and it's no wonder why.*" After a slight pause, he continued: "*And I want you all to think: how would you feel instead if your thoughts were nonstop, 'It's a lovely day, the flowers are all in bloom, I can't wait to get to work, oh, my boss has the best teeth, I just love the smell of coffee when I walk into the office—'*"

"My boss has the best *teeth?*" Kellie interrupted, incredulous. Then both women burst out laughing.

He stopped, arching an eyebrow at them. "*Yes. If everyone would think silly little things like that, you would all be so much happier. I bet you've never thought about that, have you? And a lot of your bosses do have nice teeth.*"

Still laughing, Kellie choked out, "No, I can't honestly say that I have."

"*You may think there's no reason to be grateful for your boss having nice teeth, but trust me, the way some of your bosses talk to you, if they had rotten, grisly teeth, with putrid, horrible-smelling breath, it would be much worse for you. Much worse. So don't overlook the little things to be thankful for. 'Yay, my boss uses mouthwash, I'm so lucky!'*"

Yes, you are. Think about that. There are so many little things to be thankful for that all you humans completely overlook.

"*Think about what it's like to sit down with an acquaintance of yours who complains nonstop. Usually about ten minutes of that is enough to make you want to pull your hair, bang your head, and need a bunch of aspirin. Well, you're stuck with yourself 24/7. How do you think that affects you?*"

He was really on a roll. Between his passion for the subject and their laughter, they must be quite the spectacle, Kellie thought. Slightly embarrassed, she lowered her head and quickly glanced around, looking to see if anyone was watching. The sidewalks were still deserted with no one in sight, and she breathed a sigh of relief.

He went on, "*All of you who are out there saying, 'That's not me,' I beg to differ. You just don't realize it's you. A few of you, no, it's not. But most of you, yes, it is. And it isn't only because of the daily grind of your lives, either. Even when you're on vacation, the monologue is still running: 'Can't find a gas station, the food is terrible, the room key sticks, the shower has no water pressure, the towels are scratchy, the pillows are flat, everything is so expensive, the kids won't settle down, the neighbors are inconsiderate and loud, rag, rag, rag, rag!'*"

The women broke into fresh peals of laughter.

"*You're laughing because you know it's true,*" he said. "*Both of you have been there.*"

They just nodded, still laughing.

"*And it is funny to watch. Believe me: It's very funny. You're all out there looking for more energy, but you'd have twice as much energy if you just stopped the endless negative monologue in the back of your heads. You can take all of those energy drinks, pills, herbs, and medications, or drown yourself in caffeine. Or, you could jog around the block a couple of times and turn off your mind as you do it. You'd feel a million times better. That's the energy secret right there."*

Kellie wiped the tears of laughter from her eyes and said, "I started doing Zumba three or four times a week, a few years ago. It's made a huge difference in my energy level and stamina."

He nodded. *"Good for you,"* he said. *"You found something that works for you!" So, for the rest of you, it's about whatever is going to work for you. Whatever that is, do it, as long as you can turn your mind off when you do it. It's not an easy job, I realize that. Turning off that inner critical voice is not an easy job."*

"Why is that?" Laurie inquired. "Why is it so hard for us to turn off that negative voice? You created us, so why make it so hard?"

He sighed. *"It's human nature to look at the negative instead of the positive. The negative just has a stronger pull. The soul grasps onto and holds onto the negativity. There's an edge to that negative game. There's a lot more emotion. Many, many more emotions in fact. So you hang onto it, you remember it. Part of the human game is to learn to counteract that. Remember, if everything was easy, there would be no game."* He started walking again, and they crossed the street, continuing down the beautiful flower-lined sidewalk.

"Let's go even deeper into the whole negative vs. positive question, because there's so much to be gained by understanding how this works. With all of the games to be

played, there are just as many happy, fun games as there are hard games of struggle. There are just as many easy games as hard games. And nobody's going to have a human lifetime where every aspect of the game is easy. Because when it's all easy and fun, you don't grasp the lessons."

The sidewalk began sloping downward, and they passed a charming little ice cream shop. *"I know this will be bad news to some of you. But the fact is, you humans don't grasp onto, you don't retain, and you don't appreciate the easy, gentle, peaceful games unless there's something to compare them to. In other words, you just don't 'get' the good stuff without experiencing the bad stuff, or the opposite, as well."*

"I'm not so sure about that," Laurie said skeptically. "I think I'd appreciate lots of good things coming my way just fine."

"Would you?" He said. *"Think about it. Let's say you won the lottery."* He arched an eyebrow. *"However, what you had to compare it to was giving birth to your first child last month, and buying a big beautiful custom-built home six months ago. Before that, you found your ideal job and your perfect mate. How much are you going to appreciate that lottery money? Yes, you can compare and be happy. But you won't have that thrilling, breathtaking, intense, truly life-changing feeling of 'Yay! My ship finally came in! I won the lottery! Yay!'"*

He stopped and bent down, picking up something off of the red diamond slab of sidewalk. Kellie saw it was a nice, expensive-looking man's watch, with a broken clasp.

"Someone's going to miss that and wonder where it fell off," she remarked.

"Not this time," he said. *"The owner of this watch deserves a lucky break today."*

Holding the watch in his left hand, he snapped the fingers of his right hand. With a clear bell tone, the watch disappeared. He smiled. *"He'll walk out to his car tomorrow morning and find it laying on his front walkway."*

He began walking down the gently sloping sidewalk again. *"Here's another example of the importance of contrasting experiences: Let's say you have a horrible illness, and that illness brings you down, down, down to rock bottom. You're down mentally, physically, emotionally, and spiritually. Then, through sheer determination and persistence, trying anything and everything you can, never giving up, you overcome the illness. Now you feel fabulous, spectacular, and so proud and pleased with yourself for getting to that point. You're so grateful to your doctor and to whoever helped you."*

"Yes, I know that one very well," Kellie said soberly. "You feel a lot of gratitude. I've been there."

He put his arm around her as they walked, giving her a quick sideways hug and continuing to walk with his arm resting lightly on her shoulders. *"I know you have. So you see, you need to have some of the negative with the positive, at least what you humans perceive as negative and positive. I just see it all as valuable experience. I don't have the same concept of right and wrong, negative and positive as you do. But the bottom line is that, from your perspective, there's always going to be difficulties in your lives, no matter what wonderful, great game you've chosen for this lifetime."*

"I see," Kellie said thoughtfully. "And because we're emotional beings, and the negative just has more emotion in it, it sucks us into that downward spiral more strongly."

"Yeah," Laurie said. "It's very interesting. I would never have thought about it like that."

Kellie nodded. "So we have to learn to go against what comes naturally to us then, to some degree."

They walked by a bakery with pictures of sugary confections etched on the windows. "*Yes, a lot of times, that's the game. Let's simplify it a bit. I know you and Laurie have an interest in losing weight, as do most men and women out there. So let's say you walk by a bakery.*"

He turned slightly and cocked his head toward the bakery they had just passed. "*When it's open, the tantalizing smell of baked goods is wafting out the door. Your mouth waters and your taste buds, your emotions, your entire physical bodies all crave and clamor for those brownies, cookies, and cakes.*" He snapped his fingers, and sure enough, the enticing smell of chocolate chip cookies filled the air around them. "*Or it might be an ice cream shop, where people are walking out with cones piled high with scoops of yummy-looking ice cream.*"

He used the arm around Kellie's shoulders to point back toward the ice cream shop they had passed earlier, then dropped it back down at his side. "*That's when you have to go against what your body wants. You can't just go with everything it craves, and going against that is part of the game.*"

CHAPTER 34

Kellie stopped in her tracks and turned toward him. "Ah-ha! See? Now that's another thing I just don't understand." Left hand on her hip, she pointed her right index finger at him. "I've always wondered about that. Why is it that we crave and love the things that aren't good for us? Why don't we crave vegetables? It doesn't make any sense!" She looked at him accusingly.

He stopped as well. Unperturbed, he responded: "*Because that's the game and those are the rules. You humans are great players of that one, I'll tell ya. Think about this: From the time you were a baby, what were some of the first foods or treats you were given, and what were the emotions attached to them?*"

Laurie, slightly in front of them, had stopped and turned to face them. "Ice cream," she said, eyes looking up to the right as she gave it some thought. "Cookies, candy. I used to give Ben M&M's when I was on the phone giving readings to keep him happy."

"*Exactly,*" the old man said, nodding. "*It's a delight! Parents, grandparents, all are delighted to watch the wonder and pleasure of a small child getting sugary treats.*"

It's a happy thing. What's the first birthday picture with every kid you've ever seen?"

"Blowing out the candle on a birthday cake," Kellie said immediately.

"You got it. The sugar is always a happy thing, and all kinds of happy emotions get attached to it." He pointed to Laurie. *"Laurie, in one minute or less, tell us your story."*

Obediently, Laurie began: "I've always loved chocolate chip cookie dough, because I would often make chocolate chip cookies from scratch with my grandmother. It was such a fun thing with Grandma, making those cookies. And I would eat the dough raw. I loved it back then and I still love it, because every time I eat the dough I associate the pleasant memory with it."

"Bingo," he said. *"That's the truth with so many food items people put in their mouths. It's the memory that goes with it that carries the power."*

"Yes," Kellie said, excited. "And what happens often in life is that negative emotions come up and we feel bad. And we know we can feel better if we go eat the brownie or the chocolate chip cookie dough or whatever it is, because it really does work, at least temporarily. It puts us back into that good feeling."

"And that is exactly why food is such an issue for many, many people."

Kellie shook her head ruefully. "We even justify it: 'Well, I've had a really bad day—I deserve this cookie.'"

Laurie laughed. "Have you been spying on me, Kellie?"

Kellie grinned. "Like you're the only one who ever does that. So, once again, we have to learn to go against what seems to come naturally to us. We have to go against our cravings and our bodies and our emotional desires in order to achieve our ultimate goal of being healthy and thin."

"*Yes.*"

"And, to tie that back into the current theme, if we want to have a nice, happy day, we have to do the same thing when we notice we're having negative, unhappy thoughts. We have to go against the grain and deliberately find happy, positive thoughts instead."

"*Without question.*" He turned and began walking down the street again. The women hurried to catch up and fell into step with him.

"Besides changing our thoughts," Laurie said, "what other ways can we have a nice, happy day?"

"*Good question. You humans love to help each other. You feel good when you help at work, when you help your family, your friends. Now, if you would just help yourselves the way you help others, you'd be so much happier. If you just did something nice for yourselves once a day, that would go a long, long way toward having a nice, happy day.*"

Kellie laughed. "Like having a cookie?"

"*Only if having a cookie doesn't conflict with more important goals you have, such as losing weight or becoming healthier,*" he said seriously. "*Otherwise, there's a part of you that won't feel good about it, and so you're not really doing something nice for yourself. Make sense?*"

"Totally," Kellie said promptly. "Doing something nice for yourself means doing something that makes you feel good on all levels."

"*Precisely. Now, most of you are so busy, you don't even notice your own state of mind. You're either doing what you think you're supposed to be doing or helping someone else. It doesn't even occur to you to take a few moments to do something nice for yourselves. I'm not talking about some big, grandiose thing. Just giving yourself a little thing every day would make a huge difference. Because you give, give, give to others and of course, then you're drained and tired and unhappy."*

They saw a sign advertising a travel agency just ahead. As they walked by the big window displaying pictures of cruise ships and balmy beaches with white sands and palm trees, he said, *"What you'll do is plan this big, grandiose vacation once a year to give to yourself, then you'll ignore yourself for the other fifty weeks of the year. It's crazy. I can't tell you what to do because it's different for everyone. Just think: What would please you? What would entertain you? What could you do on a daily basis to take a little time to take care of yourself? In other words, stop ignoring yourself. That's what'll make you happy."*

"Somehow our society has this notion that it's selfish to put yourself first, that you have to put everyone else before you," Kellie explained. "Moms especially tend to put their families and children first and themselves last—or, more likely, not at all. They often feel guilty for spending money on themselves or for doing anything just for them. I had to overcome that myself when my kids were young. I learned that if I didn't fill my own tank first, I had nothing left worth giving to anyone else."

"Yes, it's another game to take a look at. With all the important people, all the important things to do, where are you? Are you even on the list? Most of you haven't even made the list."

"The funny thing is," Kellie said, "When I used to coach someone with this challenge I would ask them, 'Is that how you want your children to grow up? Is that how you want them to be, always putting themselves last?' They always said no, they didn't want that. And yet, that's exactly what they were modeling."

They had come to the end of the rows of shops, and there was a grassy area to their right. He stopped and they did as well, turning to face him. He said, "*If you do just the few things we've covered, you'll be well on your way to having a nice, happy day, every day.*"

"So," Kellie said, "just to review: 'Keep your mind as clear as possible without all the negative chatter.'"

"*Check,*" he said.

"Look at the sunshine and the bright parts and be thankful for your boss's teeth, if they're great."

At the part about the boss's teeth, Laurie rolled her eyes and shook her head.

"*Check,*" he said again.

"Do something for yourself every day, make yourself important. Give to yourself, and you'll have more energy. And, you'll have more to give others. So, the next time a sexy rock star or anyone else tells you to 'Have a Nice Day,' you will!"

"*Double check. You got it.*" He gave them a big smile and two thumbs up, then walked backward onto the grass, the black leather of his outfit fading into the darkness with a small 'pop' of silver glitter.

PART VIII

WORLD CHANGES

CHAPTER 35

New York City, New York

"He won't say where we're going to meet him," Laurie said. "He just says it's a surprise." She was sitting on the floor of the living room in her new apartment, surveying all the moving boxes in various stages, from sealed and untouched to empty. The contents of the empty boxes were either spread out on the floor or already residing in their new closets or drawers.

Kellie, her voice coming out loud and clear from the FaceTime app on Laurie's phone, could tell Laurie was distinctly unmotivated to continue the onerous chore of unpacking. "Did he say when he would show up? You could take a break and get away from all that work for a while."

Laurie eyed the boxes with distaste. "I could take a break anyway."

Kellie laughed. "You could."

Laurie heaved a sigh. "He should be here any time."

It was a little over a month since they had met at the Village in Big Bear. God had come to Laurie briefly that morning and said that they were about to have their last session for the material that would go into the book they would write. The topic would be "world changes." He said they didn't need to be together in person, which was a good thing since Laurie was so busy moving and settling in. He did ask her to do her usual set-up to call him in, which she had just done with Kellie on the phone. Fortunately, distance didn't matter, so it was just as easy to surround everyone in protective white light on the phone as it was in person.

"Are you sure he didn't give you any hints at all on where we're meeting?" Kellie asked. "With such a big topic, I can't imagine where on earth we'd meet.

"I'm so curious."

"Nope. No hints. Wait—I take that back. Maybe he did. Now that I think about it, he did say, 'You're going to love the view.'"

"Well, that certainly narrows it down," Kellie said in sarcastic amusement.

Laurie heaved a sigh. "Whatever the view is, it's got to be better than the one I'm looking at right now." She reversed the phone camera so Kellie was looking at the disarray of boxes instead of at Laurie.

"*Trust me, it is.*"

At the sound of the old man's voice, Laurie whipped her head up. He was standing by the open window, silhouetted by the morning sun pouring in through the ornate wrought-iron bars.

She moved the phone so Kellie could see him. "What, now you're Peter Pan?" Laurie quipped in amusement. "You're flying in through the window?"

He grinned. "*Great idea, Laurie.*" She wasn't sure what he had been wearing before, but as he walked toward her, away from the bright light at the window, she saw that he was indeed dressed in the green tights and tunic of the famous rogue.

The outfit was complete with a soft green hat, brown feather sticking up from the back, and soft brown leather boots.

"Hey, I feel like I'm missing out on all the fun," Kellie complained.

"*Well, we can't have that,*" he said, and tossed some sparkling dust in the air. The sparkles settled into the familiar shimmering doorway, and Kellie could see it in two places: covering her bedroom doorway and behind Laurie on the phone screen as well.

The lovely hum had intermittent bell tones added this time. Kellie stepped through the doorway, appearing in Laurie's apartment.

"All *right,*" Laurie said with enthusiasm. "This is *way* more fun than unpacking!"

Kellie looked around. "I'd offer to help you unpack, but I have a feeling we're about to go somewhere much more interesting."

"*You are,*" he agreed. "*Shall we fly there?*"

"Wow, you're unusually lively today," Kellie said, raising an eyebrow. "Yeah, let's fly!"

Laurie was already on her feet. "How fun! Yes, take us flying."

"*All right. We'll fly, but as much fun as being Peter Pan is, I don't think it quite sets the right mood for our destination.*" He snapped his fingers, and with a soft chime the green outfit was instantly replaced with a shiny silver jumpsuit. Both of the women found themselves wearing the same sort of outfit. Kellie watched the material shine as she moved her arm, reflecting the sunlight from the window.

"Where *is* our destination?" Laurie asked.

But all he said was, "*Grab your shoes, Laurie, and let's go through your room and out onto the balcony.*"

They were rising in the air, backs to the sky, watching the skyscrapers of New York slowly recede.

Kellie felt no wind, just a curious sense of calm. "It's like being in an airplane, but without the plane. Plus, we're rising more vertically than a plane does."

"It feels as though we're in an insulated bubble," Laurie said, putting her arms out to either side.

"*You are,*" he said. "*You'll need it where we're going.*"

"Really? Where is that?" Kellie asked. "We're on our way, so you can tell us now."

"*Where's the fun in that? I'd rather just let you see for yourself. I'll give you another hint, though. Ready?*"

"You're having way too much fun," Kellie observed.

He laughed. "*You can never have too much fun. Okay, here's the hint: Kellie, you said, 'I can't imagine where on earth we'd meet.' I heard that, and, you were right.*"

They waited for more, but apparently that cryptic remark was it.

Kellie was about to ask for clarification, when suddenly, they sped up. Even though they were still in that insulated, calm bubble, she grabbed Laurie's arm. Faster and faster they went, continuing the upward climb without any sign of altering course or moving in any direction other than up.

And up. And up. They stared down, watching everything grow smaller and smaller, the land masses becoming more distinct and the ocean more massive as they saw more and more of it. Then they saw the curve of the earth in all directions, until finally they were so far out, they could see the entire ball that was planet Earth.

They were fascinated. The earth looked like a giant,

beautiful blue marble. The oceans, land masses, and clouds all created a lovely swirling effect. "Wow," thought Kellie, "There is no marble in existence that could rival the beauty of this." It was beyond breathtaking. They were well into space now, having left the atmosphere behind.

"Whoa," Laurie whispered. "This is fabulous! Where are you taking us?"

He said nothing but gently reached for them and turned them around so their backs were facing the earth and they were looking outward. They saw the moon then, right in front of them. Their eyes widened. They were almost to the surface. It was clearly the dark side, the craters and crags visible only by the faintly reflected light from the earth.

The silence enveloped them like a soft blanket. They were sitting cross-legged on a high platform made of the same shimmering white light as the doorway they had used so often. This time, however, it was solid, holding their weight. Altogether, it was about the size of a typical high school gymnasium floor. It looked as though it was about ten feet high in the … "Well, this is a problem in semantics," Kellie murmured under her breath. "In the air? No. In the what?" Finally, she settled on "ten feet above the surface." The white light extended upward and out far enough for them to easily see each other and a bit of their surroundings, yet it didn't affect their view of the cosmos at all.

The earth looked a lot bigger from the moon than the moon looked from the earth.

A whole lot bigger. Which was to be expected, of course; but knowing something and seeing it like this were two entirely different things. Kellie felt as though she could simply reach out and touch the gorgeous planet. It was so cool. She couldn't believe she was looking at it from this perspective. Lost in thought, she started when the old man spoke.

"I've brought you here for our last interaction for several reasons," he began. *"First, I couldn't think of a more appropriate place to discuss world changes other than here, where we can actually look at the world as a whole as we speak. From this vantage point, we should be able to see the entire globe lit up for at least the length of our session. Second, as you will see, the moon has an interesting part to play in the discussion we're about to have."*

Laurie began to say something, but the old man held up his hand to stop her. *"There will essentially be two parts to this discussion. In the first part, you may ask your questions about some of the concerns mankind has right now about the future, and I'll be happy to answer them to the degree that I can. Just remember, it's all a game, and much of the future is still to be determined. It's all going to depend on how you humans play your games. I'm sure you'd like to hear about some of the fun advances that will most certainly occur, so I'll toss in a couple of those for you, as well.*

"Then, I'm going to get to what I consider the good stuff. I'm going to talk about the advances that will occur in humans themselves and how to take full advantage of those advances. Another word for it, and the one I prefer, is gifts. It's those gifts, and what humans choose to do with them, that will ultimately determine how far, and how fast, the world progresses. So that's the plan. Are you ladies on board?"

They both nodded, still mesmerized by the gorgeous

blue marble that was Earth showcased against the deep black background of space.

"Excellent! Then let's start with your concerns. What's your first question?"

CHAPTER 36

Kellie tore her gaze away from the planet and willed herself to look at the old man. "Let's begin with the earth itself. I think most people are concerned that we're destroying it and that it won't be around for future generations. Is that true? What's in store for our planet?"

He was sitting cross-legged on the platform. He leaned forward, put his elbows on his knees, folded his hands, and rested his chin on them, piercing brown eyes looking intently into hers. *"Many humans are concerned right now with, 'How can we make money off of planet Earth?' There's no balance; that's the problem. They aren't taking care of the planet in a way that allows her to continue to thrive and to keep providing for humans. People have gotten so greedy, they are utilizing every inch of the planet without any conservation in mind at all, and it's not working.*

"This might make a few people mad, but the earth is here to supply humans. You are the most intelligent beings on the planet, and you need the most tending. Her job is to nourish you and give you what you need. However, you need to take care of the earth in order for her to continue to supply you. So go ahead: farm, fish, and drill, but allow

the earth to recover. For instance, instead of continually planting crops everywhere, allow some plots to recover.

"Ironically, taking care of the earth will bring you the most money in the long run anyway. Stripping her is very shortsighted. Think of it like this: When you're grooming an athlete, yes, you run him. But you also give him a massage and a whirlpool afterward. You take care of him. The earth would love you and give more back if you would take care of her the way you know you should. So as far as I'm concerned, the prize goes to whoever can figure out how to best pamper the earth."

"What about global warming? Laurie asked. "Everyone is so concerned and upset about that. Will it cause cataclysmic changes?" As she spoke, she turned reluctantly away from the spectacular view.

"I know everybody thinks the earth is in dire straits because of global warming, but don't worry, it will be okay. Things are heating up, yes, and part of the game is to figure out how to cool things down. Not too long from now, there will be an abundance of new energy sources discovered and created. You'll figure out how to create energy without gas, using the sun, the wind, the ocean, and more. With all the new energy available, you'll be able to work with the earth in ways you can't even imagine right now. There will be so many more ways to operate cars, heat homes, and condition the air.

"Then, as soon as you figure out how to cool things down, the game will change. I'd say in a hundred years or so, the earth will begin to go the other direction, and people will be upset because it will be cooling down. Then your game will be to figure out how to heat things up. How will you make it more comfortable and easier for humans and animals all over the world?

"The animals on Earth are more adaptable than you realize. They'll figure out how to survive in hotter climates and in colder climates as well. Most threatened species will be saved from extinction because of the efforts of humans. Saving the animals is a fun, passionate game for many people."

"What about natural disasters?" Laurie asked. "They seem to have increased in recent years, and some people are concerned about that. There's also some concern around nuclear weapons and other things that could destroy our world. What's the story on that?"

"It's true; people have noticed there seems to have been a lot of destruction and 'acts of God' such as earthquakes, floods, hurricanes, volcanoes, etc. Those have picked up slightly. However, there have always been a lot of natural disasters. What's happened is that media has become so good at reporting every incident, you're a lot more privy to what's going on in the world than you were even twenty years ago."

Kellie brought her knees up to her chest and wrapped her arms around them. "And what about man-made threats? Do we need to worry about those?"

"There won't be any big world explosions, nothing that destroys the entire world. So don't be concerned about that."

Kellie relaxed, looking visibly relieved. "Whew, that's good to hear."

"Since I have diabetes, I'm wondering about health, and what's going to happen with that," Laurie said. "Will we cure diseases like diabetes, cancer, and Alzheimer's? What about Kellie's illness, CFIDS? Will we cure that?"

"Of course, many different cancers will be cured, although not all cancer will be cured within your lifetime.

It's part of the game for people to discover cures. Cures are out there right now for some cancers, and even for diabetes if you qualify for a pancreas transplant.

"Progress will be made with Alzheimer's because of all the focus being put on it. The population in general is getting older, so it's more of a concern. More preventative measures will be discovered. Fewer people will get it. Of those who do, as soon as they are diagnosed, they'll be able to take medication that will slow its progression down tremendously.

"I don't see a cure for CFIDS, but I do see an herbal complex being developed that will definitely help. So when that herb comes out, I strongly recommend you take it, Kellie. I do not see anything helpful coming from the pharmaceutical industry.

"There is an enormous amount of research going on, and whether it's curing cancer, cramps, or stomachaches, you can see for yourself that advancements are occurring all the time and will continue to occur. Unfortunately, many advances are slowed because people are greedy and trying to make money. It's a shame when that limits what could be out there helping people. Someone needs to figure out how to make money and get the products and procedures out there.

"I will say this: You humans will legalize opting for death when you are very sick and about to die anyway. That will happen in your lifetime, so people won't have to suffer until the bitter end."

Kellie looked surprised. "I'm a little concerned about that. It seems to me it's a tough call to know where to draw the line. How sick will you have to be? What if people want to opt for death before they are really that sick and still have some quality of life?"

"The doctors will only allow it when people have been terminally diagnosed and are close enough to death, in a lot of pain, or very clearly suffering and bedridden. People won't be able to opt out just because they've had a bad week."

"But how does that fit in with your strong position on not committing suicide?" Laurie asked.

"Great question. That option doesn't count as quitting the game and taking your own life. You're about to go anyway. It will just save you a bit of unnecessary suffering at the end."

"I've heard that we're going to live longer, in general," Laurie said. "Is that true?"

"Yes, it is. Each generation will live about ten years longer than the last, on the average. So your kids will live to about 100 to 110 years of age. Tell that to them when you get home," he said, raising his eyebrows.

Kellie chuckled. "Don't most young people think they're going to live forever anyway?"

The two women were playing a fun game of low-gravity tag. With the reduced gravity on the moon, they were bouncing around on the shimmering white platform, bounding high into the air, chasing each other in slow motion. The old man aided their play with a bit of extra light, and a different harmonica note every time they hit the platform. They were careful not to bound right over the edge. He was standing at one end of the platform, looking out at the earth. Eventually, they all settled back down in sitting positions facing each other again.

"So . . ." Kellie said, a mischievous glint in her eye. "I'm ready to hear about the fun stuff. How 'bout you, Laurie?"

"I'm ready! Tell us something fun."

"*You got it. There are going to be exciting new developments in space. Humans will be living on other planets, and the moon will be first! You'll create an environment here that sustains life, and people will actually be living here.*" He spread his arms wide and looked around at the barren rocks and craters. "*What do you think of that?*"

Kellie tried to imagine rows of neat houses and streets, a small suburbia on the moon, and found it a bit challenging. "What's the time frame we're looking at here?" she asked. "In our lifetime? In our children's lifetimes?"

"*I'm looking within the next seventy-five years or so.*"

"Wow, imagine waking up to this view every morning," Kellie said with a sweep of her hand toward the blue planet. "It makes me think big, and it feels as though I have a larger perspective on things."

"I know what you mean," Laurie said thoughtfully. "It would be so cool to be a modern-day pioneer and live on the *moon!* I've heard that people might live under the ocean as well," she continued. "Will we create environments under the sea?"

"*No, that's going to be more problematic than you might think. You won't be living in the ocean any time soon. Now, here's a fun one your boys will get a kick out of: You'll be flying around in individual motorized jet packs within the next seventy-five years. In fact, those are currently in the testing phase as we speak.*"

"Cool! That's even better than living on the moon,"

Kellie said enthusiastically. "How fun will that be? Zooming to work or school in your own personal jetpack!"

"Think of all the time it will save," Laurie joined in. "No more following streets; you just fly straight there!"

"Hold on," he said, *"It won't be quite like that. Remember, all new advances will have to pass stringent safety tests and regulations first, and that's going to be a very big deal. When jet packs are legal, you'll be flying low, not high, in the air. It will be like riding a skateboard around town. You'll still have to follow the safety rules. Not everyone will opt to use them, either. Just as not everyone opts to ride a motorcycle."*

"Oh, well, it's still cool," Kellie said, undaunted.

"Glad you think so," he said. *"Now I'm ready to discuss the advances in human beings themselves. But first, why don't you two take advantage of having the best seats in the house and enjoy the view for a few minutes?"* He pointed away from the earth, where the blackness was so thick with sparkling white stars it took Kellie's breath away.

"This is spectacular," she said in amazement. "The planetarium's got nothing on this!"

"We are so lucky to get to see this," Laurie said. "Thank you for bringing us here!"

"You're very welcome. Spend some time contemplating the stars, and then we'll get down to our final business. Deal?"

"Deal!" they said together.

CHAPTER 37

fter they'd spent about twenty minutes gazing in pure wonderment at the show, he said, *"Okay, time to get down to the good stuff. Let's get started."* They turned their attention to him and waited expectantly.

"You've been so interested in what will be cured, fixed, solved, or invented," he began. *"What do you think the real key is to all of that? Who is it that's going to be doing the curing, fixing, solving, or inventing? Why, humans, of course. My job is not to make sure those things happen or even to predict them. My job is to give you humans what you need in order for you to make them happen.*

"What you need most is an advance in brainpower, and I'm giving you that gift. You'll be researching and focusing on studying the mind, learning how to access more of your brains. From here on out, you'll be able to progressively use a larger portion of your brains to come up with those cures for diseases, new sources of energy, new technologies, etc. I'm not talking about knowledge alone. You'll also learn how to access more of your ability to heal yourselves, both mentally and physically.

"A complementary gift I'm giving you is an increased interest in what you can do with your brainpower and your emotions. You'll be more curious about how you might expand yourselves. Most of you don't realize it, but sixty years ago that kind of thinking was not accepted. This acceptance of new ways of thinking is the biggest gift of all. Once you begin to develop your inner selves and your willingness to try new things, you'll enjoy greater wisdom and discover new abilities. That will give you access to much more in the way of practical and physical discoveries. It's the grandest change of all!

"World changes are really mental changes. People's minds are much more open than they've been in the past. You are becoming more interested in helping yourselves. You are beginning to realize you're not happy, and you're actively looking for how you can become happier and live more fulfilled lives. You're more open to seeking out help. You're more likely to go to psychics, therapists, and personal coaches.

"You've developed more empathy for each other overall. Many more of you are interested in becoming trained to help and heal others. Some of you will be interested in making things more pleasurable for other people. You'll be building more recreational parks, theme parks, and developing more vacation packages.

"In addition, each of you will be receiving a personal gift. No, you won't be opening your door and seeing a pot of gold. Each of you will receive a mental gift. It might be a psychic gift, it might be a healing gift, or it might be the ability to reveal the proper direction for others. It could be a gift of love, so you have more love to give others.

"Some people will receive an added dimension to their

personalities in the area of being or knowing. Others will be able to heal themselves or to heal others, mentally and physically. Many will receive the gift of intuition. More will receive a heightened ability to be compassionate, understanding, and loving of each other. Even self-appreciation and strength are gifts, and many will be receiving those.

"You all want to feel good. That's the bottom line. You want to feel peaceful, whatever your circumstances are. I want you to be aware and know that I'm making a point of helping you feel calmer and more at ease, regardless of what's going on in your lives. So if your house is flooded from a hurricane, for instance, you won't necessarily be upset. You'll see it as an opportunity to start over. You might even be excited looking at how you want to begin that new start.

"I'm helping you get there in more ways than simply offering this information. I'm giving you more opportunities to tap into your happy place. That's when the world will be more like it is in fairy tales. My vision is for you to be stargazing outside at night, and to be planting in gardens during the day with bluebirds flying around, with lots of sunshine and more peace of mind available. I want you to accept, appreciate, perceive, achieve, and experience more.

"I am hoping to expand your minds enough to create a better mind-body connection, so everyone feels much healthier and more energetic, with less need for doctors. My goal is to help you truly understand how your minds affect your bodies, so that you can avoid depression. For instance, when you have something exciting and interesting to do, you want to get out of bed. When you don't, you just want to stay under the covers. It can be that simple. If you

have something to do that you aren't excited about, then you need to lace it with something that delights you. Have your favorite breakfast, put on happy music, call a friend you love to chat with.

"However—and this is a big, big 'however'—you must realize that I can't do everything for you. I can offer the gifts, but you must take me up on them. I've already begun to give them out, and many of you aren't using them. I'm handing out abilities that are going unheeded. For instance, I'm helping people understand they have intuition, but they still aren't using it. Even though you're much more compassionate, understanding, and loving of each other, you're still holding back.

"I feel as though I hand presents to you, and you say you'll get to it later. What day of the week is later? You never get to it. Most of you don't take advantage of what's given to you.

"The only way you'll have the future you truly want is if you realize and take advantage of these gifts and talents. You each have the potential to make the world a kinder, nicer place. You're being offered the opportunity to be more compassionate and loving to each other, to get along better, and to live even longer—which is what happens when you feel contented and peaceful. The more you start acknowledging each other, complimenting and being kind to each other, and the more you tap into your goodness, the happier you'll be.

"The best place to begin is to learn to take care of yourselves better. You must first learn to do that before you take care of others. Learn to tap into your pleasure, to do more of what pleases you on all levels. That will open up your wisdom and your power. Tap into your gifts that are

talents: guitar, dance, art, and creative pursuits. So many of you don't do that. How can you give to others unless you're happy and cared for yourself?"

"That's what I used to tell my clients," Kellie said. "It's not very poetic, but what I said was, 'It's like wanting to get across town in your car and telling me you're in a hurry so you don't have time to fill up the gas tank. You'll run out of gas before you get there, and then you won't get there at all. You have to fill up your tank!'"

"It gets the point across," Laurie said. "How's this one, if you want something more poetic: 'If you want to write a winning song, you first must be inspired. So whether it's the birth of your child or a poignant break-up, something first needs to fill you with inspiration, then it can pour out of you into that beautiful song.'"

Kellie nodded. "Oh, that's good, Laurie."

"Well, I cheated," she confessed. "Archangel Metatron came up with that one and whispered it in my ear. It is good, though, isn't it?"

"It's very good."

"I don't want to put a damper on this," Laurie continued, "but so many of us really are busy and overwhelmed all the time. How are we going to find the time or the energy to tap into our talents? To write a song or to dance?"

"Lack of time and feeling overwhelmed are states of mind. They aren't real. Once you believe you have time, you will. Once you let go of the idea that you're overwhelmed, you won't be. Make it your mantra to say, 'I've got plenty of time to do everything I need to do today.' Once you've achieved caring for yourselves, it will be much easier to use your gifts to give to others.

"So, be aware that human choice is alive and well. Are

you playing with the gift I've given you? Or are you putting it in a box and shoving it under the bed? Many of you have inklings of your gift, but you brush it under the rug.

"As I've said before, I send ideas and they pop into your head clear as a bell. So don't go crawl under the covers, go to sleep, and never look at the idea again. Take action. It's up to you. Do you accept the gift? Or do you forget about it? That's part of the game of life, as you move forward. Are you aware of the gifts being handed to you? Quite often, something will happen in your life that offers you the opportunity for a beautiful, fulfilling experience. For instance, someone gets hurt or is in trouble. Are you the one to call the police or the ambulance? Or are you the one who just walks away?

"Whether it's an incident in front of you, or an idea that pops in from nowhere, do you notice, accept, and act on your opportunities? Or do you skip about your normal life acting as though nothing were different? I suggest you accept the gift and play with it. If you want to be happy and fulfilled, here's the recipe: Help yourselves first, and then help each other."

He fell silent. Laurie was staring pensively out into the starry blackness again, contemplating the old man's words, Kellie supposed. She turned away from the mesmerizing view herself and locked eyes with the old man, daring to look into their fathomless depths.

Presently, Laurie spoke up, "How can we realize more readily that you're giving us a gift? Can you put more bells and whistles on it? How can we know to pay attention to these ideas that come to mind?"

"You get little inklings. That's why meditation works. When you quiet your mind, that's when I can come in. You

need to slow down enough to quiet your mind, though. Again, you need to allow time for yourself. I'm not asking for a silent weekend. All I'm asking for is to take five minutes for yourself.

"It doesn't have to be an altered state of meditation. Just do something nice for yourself for five minutes a day. Pay attention and allow ideas to come to you. Don't do something that's distracting. Do something that will help you listen. Ask yourself, 'What message am I getting from the heavens today?'

"You humans have twice as much potential as you think you do. You have the ability to do much, much more than you realize. Every one of you has what it takes to fulfill your soul's confidence in you and play your soul cards brilliantly, creating the blissful future that is your birthright. It's all up to you: Let go of worry and stress. Understand the higher perspective of your soul. Find the opportunity in every situation. Choose to have fun and be happy. Take care of yourselves. Notice and act on your gifts, take care of each other, and your fairy tales will come true.

"I'm asking everyone—both you two, and you—the one reading or listening to these words right now: What discoveries are you going to come up with? What are you going to create? What are you going to provide to others? What will you inspire others to build, cure, solve, or invent?"

He stood up, and they both stood up with him. *"I have one last thing to say."*

He gazed lovingly at the beautiful Earth hanging like a jewel in front of them. *"I want all of you to know that I do watch over each and every one of you. So often you think I have left you. You think I'm not there, and I am. But I'm always looking at the big picture. I know the life game you chose, so I'm not going to spoil your game. I think things through, and I help you by doing what's best for you in the long run. But you're never abandoned or lost. Never. I cherish, love, and adore each and every one of you."*

The earth and stars grew bigger and brighter, then swirled magically around them in a blaze of joyous light and exquisitely beautiful music, which uplifted them and carried them home.

~ THE END ~

If you enjoyed our book and would like to tell us about it, or, if you would like more information, please visit our website at: www.playingblackjackwithgod.com

Made in the USA
Columbia, SC
17 June 2024

36712445R00152